REWRITING

REWRITING MEDEA

TONI MORRISON
AND LIZ LOCHHEAD'S
POSTMODERN PERSPECTIVES

MARIANNA PUGLIESE

Universal-Publishers
Boca Raton

Rewriting Medea: Toni Morrison and Liz Lochhead's Postmodern Perspectives

Universal-Publishers
Boca Raton, Florida • USA
2013

ISBN-10: 1-61233-259-5
ISBN-13: 978-1-61233-259-8

www.universal-publishers.com

Cover design by Leonardo Spina

Library of Congress Cataloging-in-Publication Data

Pugliese, Marianna, 1979-
  Rewriting Medea : Toni Morrison and Liz Lochhead's postmodern
perspectives / Marianna Pugliese.
      pages. cm.
  Includes bibliographical references.
  ISBN-13: 978-1-61233-259-8 (pbk. : alk. paper)
  ISBN-10: 1-61233-259-5 (pbk. : alk. paper)
  1. Medea (Greek mythology) in literature. 2. Morrison, Toni--
Criticism and interpretation. 3. Lochhead, Liz, 1947---Criticism and
interpretation. I. Title.
  PN57.M37P84 2013
  822'.914--dc23

                                                  2013011719

CONTENTS ⚜

PREFACE ❧

Ever since Euripides, the story of Medea has attracted artists and writers who have wanted to reflect on the unfathomable, mysterious nature of the maternal instinct. Medea's infanticide, read as an ambiguous and contradictory cultural act, has made her a central figure in world literature, which has constantly gone back to her in books and plays from antiquity down to the modern day.

Starting from some considerations on the symbolic significance of the Female archetype and mythological symbolism in psychoanalysis, I have tried in the opening chapter to provide some tools for interpreting the themes involving the literary figure of Medea, who is certainly the most recent chronological development of that archetype. In the later chapters I have tried to analyze how these themes have been re-used or positively re-booted in our day by Toni Morrison and Liz Lochhead. These two late-twentieth-century versions of the myth analyze not only infanticide, but other basic features of the figure of Medea, such as gender and race, in relation to the Euripidean model and in the light of the various socio-anthropological and political questions linked to the historical and social condition of these women who were redefining the contours of the story in their works.

The original plot has been rewritten and readapted, and with it infanticide has been reworked and corrected. In Euripides' tragedy infanticide was treated as principally a cruel act of revenge, and only secondarily as an act of love towards her children, while the twentieth-century re-readings, working in the shadow of feminist theory, often regard it as an act of kindness and solicitude. And so Medea becomes the loving mother of *Beloved*, who kills her children to save them from a fate crueler than death, and who, for this noble reason, can only be proclaimed innocent; or the woman with the strong foreign accent who, in Liz Lochhead, reflects the national political conscience and encourages a fresh, strong sense of cultural identity.

The characteristically male features of a dogged desire for vengeance and an obsession with striking the enemy that has humiliated and offended her so deeply, bring Medea close to the great heroes of Homer and Sophocles. She is animated and driven by virile feelings that the literary tradition had almost exclusively attributed to the heroic, strong, courageous man: in other words, the dominant male. It is precisely the male, aggressive component in her behavior, the subversive cultural element, and the ambiguity of the sexual roles in her story, that make Medea an extremely modern and significant prototype figure, whose socio-anthropological aspects continue to interest critics and infuse the twentieth-century re-writings. Aimed at illuminating the alterity of the ancient world, or seeking to universalize some features of the classical text in modern culture, the contemporary versions of the myth of Medea considered here tend to see the distinctive act of the myth – infanticide – in absolute terms as a moment of tragic retaliation, and identify Medea as a positive figure.

Unlike the system of bibliographical reference adopted for every other work cited in the text, *Beloved* by Toni Morrison will be cited by title alone. For Euripides' *Medea*, unless otherwise specified, the translation used will be that of Philip Vellacott (Harmondsworth, Penguin, 1963). For every other quote, unless otherwise specified, the translation will be mine.

I would like to thank all those who have contributed in different ways and at different times to the writing of this work, *in primis* Franca Ruggieri, without whom none of this would have been possible; Sarah Dunnigan, for her helpfulness and encouragement; my parents, to whom the work is dedicated, for their love and unconditional trust; and, last but not least, Mino, the wonderful love of my life.

INTRODUCTION 🪷

The very modernist idea of still being able to enter into debate with the tradition and establish a rapport of original creativity with it has given way in the post-modern age to the recycling of narrative material from the past in the bitter awareness of having arrived too late. For post-modern authors the relation with tradition has become just a burden to be carried, in the certainty of no longer being able to say anything that has not already been said. When the concepts of creativity and originality fail, art can no longer offer itself as ordered, harmonious form, but as a mere work of combination, re-reading and revision.

Modernist deconstruction, which offers to dismantle the logocentrism of western culture – its seeking an original, fixed meaning in the word and in reason – was, above all, the result of prizing everything that had been regarded as marginal and secondary, and in re-thinking all the binary categories of traditional metaphysics. The dichotomies of two terms with antithetical meanings and connotations – binary hierarchies in which the first term always has positive centrality, while the second is relegated to a marginal, subordinate position – were dislocated and critically reconsidered before being re-presented from a different perspective. The concept of a unitary system was violently attacked in the name of apolysemic, heterogeneous poetics: multiplicity of sense at the expense of any claim to a single interpretation of the text, though this never meant absolute arbitrariness of interpretation. Giving up the tools of thought dear to humanism and the Enlightenment meant trying to go beyond the λόγος to reach the μῦθος, not with the idea of repudiating it, but of seeking common, shareable ground with it.

Modernist deconstruction was always accompanied by the desire to construct new narrative paradigms. Post-modernist texts, by contrast, emerge from fusing scraps of texts from the past and adroitly assembling citations drawn from the most disparate sources. While there was still a strong desire to break with the past in modernist experimentation, as well as the need to create new forms that could interpret reality, the parodies and pastiches[1] of post-modernism are dominated by the game of combining the parts that have been assembled and that are always open to infinite, hybrid exchanges of mutual assimilation. Yet, a citation produces an extremely original relation between the text and its model: in the process of revision, the original text is so deeply assimilated to the new one that any distinction between copy and original is no longer possible[2].

Linda Hutcheon, who has thought long on the characteristics of post-modernist writing (1985: 11 and ff), sees parody and the overturning of models as some of its fundamental elements. The poetics of the second half of the twentieth century gave the categories of modernity a radical and relativist rethink, the concept of sense becoming plural and expressing itself in dissonance and fragmentation. The relation between what Genette calls hypotext and hypertext (1982) – between the text and its model, between source and citation – becomes the element that gives back meaning to writing. The direct line of descent is broken and new perspectives open up the text in new directions of sense; writing becomes an open, polyphonic space, in which the relation of reverent or irreverent subordination to the model gives way to a relation of total freedom, in which, as Borges recalls, it is now the writer who shapes his precursors, his work modifying the conception of both past and future (1963: 108).

No writer's work can be judged by and in itself; we need to understand it in its relation to its predecessors, and place the author in an already existing order that was concluded before the new work appeared, but which can be subverted or modified with its arrival. The continuity between old and new lies precisely in the new balance that has just been found: anyone who shares this idea, noted T.S. Eliot, will not be surprised to see the past modified by the present just as much as the present is inspired by the past[3]. Literature has

---

[1] In his canonical essay on literature in the second degree (*Palimpsests*, 1982), Genette makes a sharp distinction between parody and pastiche: the former consists in the transformation of a single text, while the latter in the imitation of a class of texts.

[2] In fact, one of the first definitions of pastiche was that of a hybrid work, halfway between copy and original. (See Hoesterey, 2001, chap. I).

[3] «No poet, no artist of any art, has his complete meaning alone. His significance, his appreciation is the appreciation of his relation to the dead poets and artists. You cannot value him alone; you must set him, for contrast and comparison, among the dead» (*Tradition and the individual talent*, 1922: 49).

always fed on literature, and takes form in the relation that texts enjoy with the other texts that have preceded them. This is the idea of «intertextuality» (Kristeva, 1980) as an open system of citations that make of the new text a dynamic, changing place in which the word denies and recreates, re-codifies and re-establishes, and is fully defined and understood[4].

In this scenario, the intertextual relation that twentieth-century literature re-established with Greek drama became particularly profound, given the alterity and remoteness of the earlier cultural system. New anti-totalitarian modes of experience and writing were sought that would not be enslaved by the model, but would be part of an unceasing dialogue between equals. The awareness that literary truth can only exist in intertextuality – in the multiplicity of texts that make it up – withdrew myth from the coercive referential reality of the event and projected it into an alternative reality in which we can distance ourselves from the mythical happening and the primary text that represents it, recreating it in a narrative game that involves and implies the author's subjectivity. No longer conditioned by reverence and imitation, the relation with the classics became more complex, expressing the need to say again what may already have been said, but to always include a gap, and always reveal a difference.

The dialectic relation between text and model further benefited from contributions from other fields, such as psychology and anthropology, and other artistic genres, such as the cinema and the theatre, which have brought the ancient world closer and helped it reverberate in the constraints of the present. Disciplines that were originally far removed from critical and literary practice *tout court*, like Marxism and psychoanalysis, began to be applied to literary themes and motifs, playing a fundamental role in focusing and defining a genuine thematic criticism[5].

The initial championing of difference gradually gave way to a hybrid vision of identity, at which point literary theory – from feminist criticism to Afro-American studies – could show how close-knit was the texture of social discourses with which literature interacts. The literary text became a means by which one could elaborate a concept

---

[4] Julia Kristeva re-christened Bachtin's dialogism with the technical term, intertextuality (1975: 445-482).
[5] Yet, it must be admitted that, for all the efforts of literary theorists, it is almost impossible to find a single definition for this discipline and establish an apparatus of canonical rules to delimit it.

of cultural, ethnic and sexual identity, conceived as a social, and therefore composite and mutable, construction. The myth of Medea, more than others, seems to intercept some of the most pregnant themes in contemporary culture, particularly the contrast between ethnocentrism and cultural relativism, the recent post-colonial debate and the speculations of feminist theory; and it is that which explains its extraordinary popularity.

But we must make a quick distinction between the relation with the myth and the relation with the primary text that represents it: in the specific case of Medea, with Euripides. Twentieth-century artists, with tirelessly prolific creativity, often tended to supplant the ancient text and re-shape the myth directly, often going back to its most archaic forms. In this way, the myth became the equivalent of a literary theme, one that could be dismantled into various thematic nuclei that, one by one, could proliferate further themes.

In this sense, Freudian aesthetics has made an important contribution to thematic criticism: after the ostracism it had suffered in the years of Structuralism, it has recently been revalued, to the point of having acquired a respectable position in literary criticism[6]. The great discovery that the unconscious has a logic and a language of its own, and that it can therefore be systematically interpreted despite the apparent illogicality of its manifestations, was exploited by the great artists who, in Freud's wake, distorted the most intimate, primary fantasies and dressed them up in literary clothing. The identification and interpretation of the themes in the works of an author were not limited to the sphere of intentional hermeneutics, but extended to the fascinating and terrible horizons of the unconscious. In this sense, thematic criticism established a profound relation with psychoanalysis and the pre-symbolic area of the consciousness where *reverie* – an author's poietic activity – begins. It transcended the false conception of analytic theory as no more than a hymn to the freeing of unconscious, repressed drives, and its contribution to literary criticism, particularly in its numerous studies of the imagination and the symbolism of myths and the extra-literary significance of archetypes, has continued to be strongly felt in recent times. Although it has been modified by later schools and attacked by cultural studies,

---

[6] For bearings on thematic criticism, see D. Giglioli (2000) *Tema*, Florence, La Nuova Italia, W. Sollors (ed), (1993) *The Return of Thematic Criticism*, London, Harvard University Press, and C. Segre, *Tema / Motivo*, in *Avviamento all'analisi del testo letterario*, (1985) Torino, Einaudi.

Freudian aesthetics continues to be inexhaustibly suggestive for those who want to attempt a diachronic explanation of the presence of the same themes and myths in different ages and different cultures.

The various motifs of a myth are linked to the principle moments in the history of its reception, and, so, to the various authors who have salvaged them by remixing the quantities: Euripides, who was the first to fix Medea as the literary prototype of the conscious and deliberate murderous mother; Seneca, fascinated by the supernatural character of the witch of Colchis, whose traces would be followed by renaissance and baroque writers; and then the authors of the nineteenth and twentieth centuries, from Grillparzer onwards, who tended to respond to the barbarian from the East who acts out her tragedy as a foreigner living in Greece. These *topoi*, which, respectively, represent the figure of the woman in love, devastated by the overwhelming power of eros; the demoniac figure linked to the superhuman dimension of witchcraft and magic; and the barbaric foreigner from the distant East who arrives in a strange and hostile land, were the basic themes of the myth, which became frames of cultural reference.

The myth of Medea is retold in the light of one of its thematic centers: placed center-stage, it is offered as an explanation of the infanticide, which, in a psychoanalytic perspective, is an example of Kleinian envy. The children are killed because, through them, she really wants to attack someone else – to be precise, the father who generated them. Sacrificing them allows Medea to genuinely interrupt her husband's line of descent, depriving him of his heirs by the infanticide, and symbolically interrupting his happy life by a vicarious substitution that satisfies her desire for vengeance. In the last analysis, the mother ends up turning on her child the aggression and conflict that she actually feels for the father, and that both external circumstances and her own inner dividedness prevent her from turning directly against him. In this way the child becomes the means to create suffering for or attract the attention of the person who is the real object of her hostility. Her hatred for the man who has betrayed and abandoned her is directed at the child who is the physical embodiment of the fruit of the union and is, for the mother, certainly a less fearsome antagonist.

However, in the infanticide's gesture we might glimpse the mother's hallucinatory desire for total possession of her children, with the obvious exclusion of the father, almost as if the child had been generated by parthenogenesis. In this sense, Medea's act would seem perfectly explicable, in obviously unconscious terms, as the need to retake possession of what is perceived as her own and that is actually experienced as total possession by the other. In this case too, the killing of the children coincides with the exclusion of the father figure from a deep, intimate relation that is the exclusive experience of the mother and her offspring. The all-absorbing bond between them is re-established through the symbolic return of the child to the maternal womb; in any case, the mother's re-appropriation of her children happens at the paradoxical price of their death.

The affinity between feminism, post-modernism and psychoanalysis consists precisely in its resistance to a fixed, and often stereotyped, identity, such as, for example, the equation Medea/murderous mother: the theme of the lack or loss of identity, which is often combined with that of physical monstrousness or sexual ambiguity, is frequent in contemporary female re-writings, and confirms the importance of the transfiguration of characters in the literary scene. A relation with tradition, which is in any case problematic and difficult, was historically precluded to women. Regarded as endemically weak and subaltern beings, their complex existence was for centuries recounted through often deceptive images created by the male culture that ended up taking the place of their deeper reality. The desire to fill this void and build on the ruins of the past a legitimate tradition of their own that might illuminate the shadowy areas of Western culture and at the same time free female creativity by exploiting their subjectivity, opened a debate about revising the prescriptive concepts of tradition and canon. Rejecting codified forms and genres, and starting from their position as outcasts, women therefore made difference the center of both their narrative and their poetics. And so ideological criticism of patriarchal thinking, on which the traditional idea of literature was based became the theme of a new form of writing that argued against, and offered a concrete alternative to, this thinking. Literature confronted existence and, opposing the ideological officialdom of power in all its forms, created effective strategies for repeating what had already been said – but subversively; using gender clash to examine significant moments of social life, literature became a hermeneutic tool of the present.

After centuries of a pitiless, diabolic Medea, the twentieth-century re-readings of the myth, particularly those by women, took a different path Euripides and Seneca, offering alternative solutions that were often mirror images of them. These re-readings of the myth by women seem particularly significant as they produce a new echo of the original that resounds unfamiliarly, with surprising effects.

And so Euripides' Hellenization of the savage Medea became an anti-colonialist, anti-modernist, anti-Western assimilation of the barbarism and alterity of the foreigner, while Seneca's witch became a good, powerful healer. The crisis of the λὸγος, typical of much of post-Enlightenment modern culture, therefore found itself in accord with the story of the barbarian woman who, because of her ethnic diversity, is deranged by her meeting with the Greek hero and the culture he represents. In the two re-readings presented here, the myth of Medea becomes, respectively, a political tool to denounce colonialism and overturn the dominant categories, and a revalued anthropological model of a barbarism that should be assimilated and sublimated by modernity; in both, the exaltation of a pre-symbolic vital force that calls up our ties with the Earth and the mystery of existence.

Freed of any frame of reference, the new voices of the women who write and re-write the myth move forward like unfettered slaves who have at last stopped seeing themselves in terms of their origins, and can set up a dialog that releases them from solitude and isolation. The killing of a child by a mother was, and remains, the subversive gesture *par excellence* in relation to the norm or reality expected by the collective imagination; in doing it, the person concerned, the mother, as woman, re-confirms her abjectness *par excellence*. Needing to redeem the figure of Medea and, so, restore her dignity and depth against all the prejudices that have relegated her over the centuries to the status of a terrible murderess, authors such as Liz Lochhead and Toni Morrison have rehabilitated her, wholly or in part, as a social and mythical subject, giving her a new position in the secular dimension of history through the timelessness of myth.

CHAPTER ONE

Medea: Symbolic Implications of the Myth

1. The Myth: Oral Tradition and Literature

Finding a satisfactory definition of myth is no easy task, but, as the etymology of the word suggests, myth is a transmitted narrative, a traditional story: for the ancient Greeks μῦθος was simply the «word», the «story», almost a synonym for λὸγος or ἐπος, with the simple difference of being neither directly nor rationally demonstrable –indeed, completely unverifiable. Yet, myth's claim to truth, which, as truth, fulfills a social and collective function and is understood as a genuine moral story, follows from its intention to tell a story that is fundamentally sacred and universal.

In other words, a myth tells how, thanks to the deeds of supernatural beings, the cosmos, or a part of it, came into being. It is the narrative of a creation, of how something was produced or began to be, of how a part of inchoate reality became an object through the attribution of a name, and of how man then tried to explain to his reason its profoundly unfathomable nature. It provides an explanation and also a guarantee of the validity of the elements that make up the social, intellectual and moral patrimony of a culture: it projects into a more or less distant past the psychological needs of a society, setting them in a sacred context that legitimizes it. Paraphrasing Hans Blumenberg (1991: 25-58), a myth is the primitive elaboration of man's fear, the result of exorcizing his existential anguish and mastering the episodic 'tremenda' of recurrent cosmic phenomena. A myth is therefore a metaphor, something that is «placed before» the object of direct action, to keep at bay or simply weaken what humans sense as an uncontrollable danger.

The product of an archaic mentality, myth is often dominated by magic thinking: things, animals and natural phenomena seem to be animated and humanized, and metamorphoses of every kind are possible in it; gods, heroes and men come together as a single whole in which the sacred and the profane act in absolute continuity. A myth is a narrative of fantastic and legendary events about divinities and ancient heroes or relations between man, nature and what is supernatural, and it is in some way linked to religious beliefs. Myths probably derived from the need to provide universal answers to the human questions about the mysteries of the cosmos and life, embodying natural phenomena, historic events and states of mind in concrete, palpable figures that can mirror the human condition. Myths, like fables, have been interpreted as the creation of a primitive humanity endowed with a lively imagination, but, unlike fables, they are not just tales of pure imagination: they have a sacred character and so require an act of faith. They are, above all, truth, or a way of approaching the truth that is particularly valid when we are entering regions not susceptible to exploration by rational thought.

Through narrative, then, myth seeks to reveal universal being, and for this reason it can be presented as a sacred story whose very origins are supernatural; the telling of a myth releases a message whose origin is lost in the mists of time and space: a message that comes from no specific sender, and for this very reason soon becomes part of tradition. Yet, every myth requires a means of transmission that, sooner or later, is fixed in more or less definitive written versions. At this point literature intervenes as the authentic keeper of the myth, which, otherwise, would often be lost and, so, unknowable. What would have become of Ulysses without Homer, or Oedipus without Sophocles? The myth always reaches us in the mantle of literature, becoming in turn literature itself.

In his essay on methodology entitled *Les Etudes de Thèmes* (1965) Raymond Trousson thought he could recognize a literary theme whenever a motif that seemed like a concept or an intellectual construct was fixed and defined in one or more characters, and whenever these characters then gave life to a genuine literary tradition. Like many other mythical figures, then, Eteocles and Polynices, Oedipus and Medea should be regarded as literary themes rather than literary myths, illustrating, respectively, the opposition between two brothers, incestuous love, and the betrayed barbarian who becomes a murderous mother. Yet, there is striking divergence among scholars in attributing meaning to these basic semantic units in the literary texts which can be called themes or motifs. In general, we tend to regard a motif as a smaller thematic unit, which represents an element of content, a situation that is part of the narrative totality of a story, which is generally identified as the theme. For Ceserani, Domenichelli and Fasano (2007) the two terms are not subject to precise definition and are interchangeable. Although authors such as Cesare Segre (1985) and Elizabeth Frenzel (1962, 1976) have tried to give complete definitions of the two terms, the terminology has remained fairly tangled, and the difficulty in reaching an agreed definition of theme has remained fundamentally unsolved.

In recognizing the principle of the universality of myth in the adaptability of some of its constituent elements[7], thematological studies define the relation between mythology and literature in terms of a fertile re-codification of the narrative material that, moving in different expressive codes, modifies its own textual status and is transformed from an ethno-religious tale into a genuine literary text. Only then would we want to call it a real literary myth, in the sense of a narrative that the author can freely manipulate and transform, giving it new meanings that bring out most fully its dynamics for that age.

The polysemic and universal nature of myth, which allows it to be constantly re-functionalized and to find itself at home in any age, is determined precisely in the intersection between mythical story and cultural history. The presence of ethno-religious myth in literature comes about through a process that Genette describes as transformation rather than imitation (1998: 7, 8) – that is to say, through the re-codification of the narrative material, which originated outside literature but is not extraneous to literature's creative processes. This process of transformation requires creative and often original intervention on the hypotext, in the course of which various interpretations can be adopted that more or less radically transform the hypertext in making the hypotext newly relevant, and therefore make possible innumerable rewritings of the myth and innumerable variations.

2. The Female and the Great Mother

In seeking to interpret the rewriting of the myth of Medea as a wholly female experience – of the heroine herself and of the three authors of these daring transpositions of the myth – I have had to make

---

[7] Kerenyi defines these aspects as archetypal models that, when enhanced with elements of a given culture, give rise to myth. Specifically, he speaks of «mythologem», which is the mythical material that is constantly reassessed, remodeled and shaped, like an endless river of images (1969: 15).

some remarks on the archetype of the Female which the mythical figure of Medea, the terrible mother, certainly calls up. Consequently, I have been unable to ignore the description of the Female, in the sense of a universal principle present since the most distant times, which Erich Neumann and analytical theory have provided in relation to the importance of the Archetype in the psychic life of the individual and in the collective unconscious[8].

In *The Great Mother* (1955) Erich Neumann sees the *Female* Archetype as having an *elemental character* and a *transformative character*. The *elemental character* is the aspect that tends to keep everything that arises from and is contained in the female fixed and immobile. The elemental character's tendency to conserve, which has generally positive associations and is expressed in functions such as nurturing, offering protection and warmth, contrasts with the transformative character of the Female, an often negative expression of movement and change, novelty and transformation.

Both these characters, however, are carriers of the ambivalence that is typical of the Female Archetype, and of every Archetype in general, which, with a shift as sudden as it is paradoxical and inexplicable, allows positive and negative phenomena to be confused in an indistinct, ouroborean fusion[9], reminiscent of the still undifferentiated primordial archetype. The Archetype's dynamism allows a phenomenon to shift into its opposite in ways incomprehensible and mysterious to the consciousness, which dissolves before its luminous fascination and so is unable to discriminate. «The tendency to relativize opposites is a notable peculiarity of the unconscious» (Jung, 1981: 36), which works by symmetries and generalizations[10], with no respect for the logical principle of identity and non-contradiction formulated by Aristotle in his *Metaphysics*. The archetype is an inner image, invisible and indescribable, a pre-existing mythological presence in the collective unconscious, universally known because intimately human.

---

[8] See also Jung (1956, 1981).

[9] The *Ouroboros*, symbolized by a circular serpent eating its tail, «*is the symbol of the original psychic situation, in which man's consciousness and ego are still small and undeveloped*» (Neumann, 1981: 29).

[10] See Matte Blanco, *The Unconscious as Infinite Sets* (1975), in which he adds eight more characteristics of the unconscious to the five already formalized by Freud, tracing them back to two fundamental principles: that of symmetry and that of generalization.

The primordial image, the primordial symbol[11], then, is simply perceived by the unconscious and not yet thought or transformed into a concept by the consciousness: essentially mythical and instinctual, the primeval image can be faithfully represented only in the language of images and symbols. The positive elemental character of the Female, in Neumann's sense of a nature that generates and nourishes, protects and warms, deriving from the most immediate human experience – what we can see in the relation between mother and child – is flanked by the elemental negative character of the Female, more hidden and less evident, that derives from an inner experience, secret and unconscious, yet equally significant in constructing the Female archetype. So negative features too have a role in defining the Female and the maternal: «danger and distress, hunger and nakedness, appear as helplessness in the presence of the Dark and Terrible Mother» (Ibid: 149). Thus life and death, birth and destruction, are intimately linked with each other; and that is why Neumann calls this fearsome, terrifying Female «Great».

The first great manifestation of the powerful, limiting hostility of the Great Mother manifests itself when the elemental, solicitous protection of the womb gives way to expulsion into the transforming world, an event as necessary as it is violent and traumatic. The first great rejection by the mother is felt by every individual at the moment of birth: and being born thus becomes the cause of every ill[12]. If birth is perceived by the new-born «as a rejection from the uterine paradise» (Neumann, 1981: 68), what makes birth possible – pregnancy – is the first way in which the mother can probe her transformative character. The woman transforms both her body and her child's, and this transforming character therefore appears from the start as «connected with the problem of the *thou* relationship» (ibid: 31), the dialectic relation with what is other than oneself. In fact, it seems that the maternal instinct is not a universal feeling, but develops only secondarily in a woman, when it brings advantages and can

---

[11] The function of the symbol in this sense is indicated by its etymology: σύμβολον<σύμ-βάλλω, I put together).

[12] «Nasce l'uomo a fatica, ed è rischio di morte il nascimento. Prova pena e tormento per prima cosa; e in sul principio stesso la madre e il genitore il prende a consolar dell'esser nato». (G. Leopardi, *Canto notturno di un pastore errante dell'Asia*, 1831), («Man struggles to be born, and birth is the risk of death. The first thing he feels is pain and anguish; and from the very start his mother and father console him for being born»).

act usefully. Maternal love is not so much a primary instinct, as the consequence of the establishing of a relation, or rather the feeling that grows up in a relation. Not nature, then, but experience and the socio-cultural context of experience, develop a mother's feeling for her offspring: the first and most instinctive reaction of the mother when faced with her new-born baby is often that of rejection and repulsion.

In Neumann's view, the development of patriarchal values meant also a cultural bias in favor of consciousness – and the male gods of light and the sun – at the expense of the archetype of the Female, the personalization of primordial semi-goddesses like Circe or Medea reducing them to little more than wicked witches, their power and splendor debased. As a result, the negative dimension of the Archetype now seems primordial or unconscious, and the unconscious is symbolized as feminine. The unconscious, like the moist, subterranean world of the woman's womb and the belly of the earth, shapes, generates and transforms, and for this reason it is symbolically female. In a numinous, symbolic place, secret and archetypal, then, «anguish, horror and fear of danger» (Ibid: 147) are hidden, and the fecund womb of the mother and the earth becomes the deadly, devouring uterus of the tomb.

Thus, to be able to understand and visualize the horror of such an inhuman, terrifying anguish, and to try to explain how much more *monstrous*[13] it seemed to him, man[14] had to resort to mythical images with which he could exorcize his fear: and so, fantastic, chimerical female images[15], from the Gorgons to the Erinyes, from the Furies to

---

[13] The adjective «monstrous» >lat. *monstrum* (what is presented, what is manifest, visible) refers to what surprises in its presenting itself, what fascinates and frightens at the same time, as well as the wonder and disquiet when faced with what is not immediately understandable or verifiable.

[14] In this connection see Patrizia Adami Rook, *Le due Femminilità: la crisi della coscienza femminile nel sogno e nel mito* (1983) where, in sharp contrast with Neumann's theory, the author claims that the Great Mother and the Female are specifically male unconscious images and not human in the wider sense; they are simply some of the many representations of woman made by man, and so cannot be regarded as Archetypes or self-depictions of the Female.

[15] Yet, representations of the Terrible Mother often possess phallic characteristics and male attributes that make them still more fearsome in their castrating power and make her an almost bisexual or sexually amorphous being. Citing some examples taken from the pre-Greek world (3500-1750 BCE), we need only recall the Gorgons, with their boar's tusks, and the

Medusa, embody in their fascinating monstrosity and the menacing forms of witches, magicians and vampires, the most intimate, obscure, fearsome and powerful side of the Female.

3. The Mystery of Female Fluids: Weakness Becomes Strength

The transformative, creative character of woman, which is fundamentally disquieting, negative and uncontrollable, therefore seems all the more disturbing, the more it appears to be intimately connected with the deep-seated mysteries linked to the blood: menstruation, pregnancy and the production of milk. The woman is an uncontainable mass of emotions and contradictions, of devastating drives and messy, confused fluxes that need to be held back in the chaos from which they arise. In this sense, the phantasm of fluids, which analytical theory has reflected on extensively (Freud, 1905 and Klein, 1957, 1975b), tries to explain the irresistible power of female excitement by identifying a subtle link with the fluid emissions that burst from the woman's body in the same overwhelming and uncontrollable way.

The woman, whose sexual being displays deficiency[16], the result of an atavistic, congenital deprivation, seeks to fill this great void of hers with the inexhaustible *more* of the other sex, or to compensate her lack with the too much of herself, which thus becomes excess and overflowing. Eternally inscrutable and mysterious, strange, and, so, seemingly hostile (Freud, 1918), she risks contaminating the man with her femininity, and it is this that frightens him[17].

---

snake-haired Medusa: teeth, like snakes, are certainly symbols of the destructive nature of the Female, as well as qualities almost exclusively connected with male power.

[16] According to analytical theory, a woman's sexual identity is determined by an initial emasculation. The castration complex, or rather, the «female masculinity complex», as Freud himself redefined it in the *The Dissolution of the Oedipus Complex* (1924), derives from the woman's renewed fear of being deprived of her penis, imagining she possessed it before losing it by castration. (Freud, *Some Psychical Consequences of the Anatomical Distinction Between the Sexes* (1925), *Female Sexuality* (1931), *The Interpretation of Dreams*, (1899), *The Sexual Enlightenment of Children* (1907), *On the Sexual Theories of Children* (1908), *Three Essays on the Theory of Sexuality*).

[17] The complex of female castration becomes a genuine fear of castration in a man, who fears losing his penis, usually because of a female figure, as once again a possibility in the future.

> A male immature in his development, who experiences
> himself only as male and phallic, perceives the Feminine
> as a castrator, a murderer of the phallus [...] intensifies
> the terrible character of the Feminine. Thus the Terrible
> Goddess rules over desire and over the seduction that
> leads to sin and destruction; love and death are aspects of
> one and the same Goddess. (Neumann, 1981: 172)

The memory or the renewal of the threat of emasculation «arouses a terrible state of emotion in [the boy] and forces him to believe in the reality of the threat which he has hitherto laughed at. This combination of circumstances leads to two reactions, which [...] will [...] permanently determine the boy's relations to women: horror of the mutilated creature or triumphant contempt for her» (Freud, 1925: 251). The woman's strength arises precisely from her weakness and absence: yet, corresponding to her lack of sperm will be her production of milk, and her turgid and excretory breast will make her so unattractively phallic and fearsome in the eyes of a man that she will become a real threat to him. Milk, then, no longer seen as merely nutriment for the child, but as orgasmic fluid of sensual pleasure and power, of force and vitality, feeds the man's castration fear, his terror of being emasculated by a plausible *«other»*, with whom he needs to compete, if he is to survive. In addition, as he can only be born but cannot give birth to a new creature, he remains fixed in the first moment of his birth, that single happy event on which any attempt on his part to rejoin his mother will depend, until death alone allows him to recover the original oneness by returning to the darkness that had generated him.

Only women give birth, and the male cannot grasp the sense of this specific mode of being. Being a mother is a wholly female way of being, unknown to the man, who seeks in vain to understand its mystery, just as he tries in vain to resist the deadly rage of which a woman is capable when she decides to avenge a wrong done her. The power and mystery of creation are female, numinous secrets, before whose obscurity the man can only withdraw helpless.

Being born means separating, managing to detach oneself from the mother so as to be able to exist: but giving birth means having to separate, and for this reason it is doubly painful. In giving birth, a woman dies and is reborn, because she becomes a mother and knows what it means to experience separation as a moment necessary for the *individuation*[18] of the new being. Nevertheless, she has none of her creature's dejection, but only the omnipotence and force of the creator, able to destroy her creature without hesitation or pity. «When the mother goddess avenges herself, the female will not allow herself to be fertilized, or she aborts her fruits» (Adami-Rook, 1983: 59); she is willing to repeat the sacrifice and destroy the fruits of her own womb, thus becoming the mythical monster-hero in which every woman can recognize herself and from whom she can learn (Eliade, 1958).

> The archetypal relationship between death and birth is intensified by their symbolic connection with loss and sacrifice, and fertility forms a unity with sacrifice of the phallus, castration and blood. (Neumann, 1981: 202)[19]

Paraphrasing Sheridan Le Fanu, there can be no bloodless sacrifice, and the sacrifice required by any act of love, any act of creation – whether physical or artistic – is necessarily a blood sacrifice[20].

4. The Ambivalent Nature of Milk

Like writing, breast-feeding is such a carnal experience that it cannot be forgotten, either by the child or by the mother. The child will go on yearning for a woman's breast in future, as it will remind him of a pleasure he has already experienced; while the mother, who in certain forms of depression connected with weaning identifies the baby as a vampire, prolongs the breast-feeding, almost as if she wanted to put off forever the moment of a fundamentally impossible separation.

The Great Mother returns with all her cannibalistic power to devour her children, in a primal, indistinct desire for self-preservation (Freud, 1914), and the drives of the Ego, whose only end is the preservation of the individual, ride roughshod over the sexual drives, which aim at the preservation of the species. Considering the classic split between a «good» breast, which feeds and protects, and a «bad»

---

[18] Actually, woman escapes the *principium individuationis* as her body is not etymologically «in-dividual» , though it can become two from one.
[19] See also Freud, 1905.
[20] «Love will have its sacrifices. No sacrifice without blood» (Le Fanu, J. S., 2000: 123).

breast, exciting and corrupting, we cannot fail to identify a subtle correspondence between the distinction, cited above, and that already described between the elemental character and the transformative character of the Female.

A woman whose transformative character is dominant is a woman who has become capable of a genuine relation with what is other than herself, that is to say, with the partner through whom she can generate life and contain it again inside her body. The distinction, presented like that, clearly refers to that between what is female and what is maternal, if a separation of this kind is possible, and, far from being clear and simple, it is still not wholly resolved: the so-called «bad» breast – the breast of sexual drives – is not an object for the lover's exclusive pleasure, but rather, and not without complications, exciting and pleasure-giving for both the suckling baby and the mother.

Thus, breast-feeding becomes an experience that is not just narcissistic, but profoundly erotic. Freud had already underlined the erotic aspect of breast-feeding; but, saying nothing about the sexual sensations of the woman who breast-feeds, he had merely described the exciting effect of breast-feeding on the child. He wrote:

> Sensual sucking involves a complete absorption of the attention and leads either to sleep or even to a motor reaction in the nature of an orgasm; [...] Furthermore, it is clear that the behavior of a child who indulges in thumb-sucking is determined by a search for some pleasure which has already been experienced and is now remembered. In the simplest case he proceeds to find this satisfaction by sucking rhythmically at some part of the skin or mucous membrane. It is also easy to guess the occasions on which the child had his first experiences of the pleasure which he is now striving to renew. It was the child's first and most vital activity, his sucking at his mother's breast, or at substitutes for it, that must have familiarized him with this pleasure. (Freud, 1905: 179)

The difficulty felt by society, and by the woman *in primis*, to reconcile the function of breast-feeding as the disinterested result of maternal love, and the pleasure deriving from the stimulation of the breast considered as a source of *libido* for the mother too, has meant that the opposition between maternity and sexuality has remained unresolved to this day. Yet, the contradiction between the breast that nourishes and the breast that gives pleasure, between what is maternal and what is female, between the sensual current and the tender current of the libido (Freud, 1912), is only an apparent one, and refers rather to the opposition between what the breast itself ambivalently contains in itself: the turgid flesh that forms it and makes it so sexually desirable, and the fluid that holds and that impoverishes it, spoils it and weakens it, whenever it is extracted from it.

The opposition is well-known to the small child, who establishes equivalences between all the substances of the body (Klein, 1975b) and clearly separates solid objects, such as the breast, the penis and feces, from fluid substances, such as milk, tears and sperm. Fluids, and water in particular, define and distinguish the woman, to the extent that, in the words of Mircea Eliade, «The Waters symbolise the entire universe of the virtual; they are the *fons et origo*, the reservoir of all the potentialities of existence; they *precede* every form and *sustain* every creation.» (Eliade, 1997: 151). Water, in fact, purifies and regenerates; it disintegrates forms and eliminates any structure, washes sins away and opens the way to a new life. «Everything that has form manifests itself above the Waters, by detaching itself from them. On the other hand, as soon as it is separated from the waters, [...] every form comes under the laws of Time and of Life; it acquires limitations, participates in the universal becoming, is subject to history, decays away and is finally emptied of substance» (ibid.: 152).

Milk, like water, is above the forms of any structure; like water, it participates in the unfathomable mystery of life. Since ancient times, milk, almost as if it could never be reduced to its strict physiological components, had been regarded as an unsettling fluid, a strange female product closely linked with blood, and with menstrual blood[21]. A strange fluid, whose powers and risks are certain, disturbed by sexual desire and altered by menstruation, milk remained, over the centuries, the fluid product of the creature that was more formless than any other: woman. The woman, the mother, is, indeed, amor-

---

[21] According to the haemogenetic theory of milk and semen, which was held unquestioningly throughout the Renaissance, but which had already been set out by Aristotle, Hippocrates and Galen, milk and sperm both originated from the blood. Yet women, more than men, managed to blanch the blood and turn it into milk, thanks to the different capacity of the blood vessels to heat the blood.

phousness *par excellence*: she is wholly made up of insatiable fluidity, an interplay of gushing fluids hidden in the moist depth of a dark, fluid matrix. And the breast, so fragile and so powerful in its aesthetic and sexual form, becomes a mere solid container of a fluid substance that gives nutrition and life, but that might unexpectedly and uncontainably overflow.

Milk, then, like the other female fluids, bursts out with the violence of a basic drive: like blood and tears, it overflows in a recalcitrant excess that is inherent in woman's very nature and that man nevertheless feels the need to control. This excess, which is almost exclusive to the female essence, manifests itself mainly in the interplay of fluids, connected with each other in a precarious, fundamentally unstable, balance, as well as in all the phases of the female sexual life: woman, in fact, from puberty to pregnancy, from birth to breastfeeding, undergoes the violence at work in her body and lives through the eternal sickness of being a woman.

Woman, fragile and anemic, whom menstruation kills, childbirth drains and breastfeeding vampirizes, is the sick being *par excellence*, a restless, uncontrollable body, morbid and monstrous, at once omnipotent and fragile, that becomes the source of pleasure and destruction, of life and death, in an alternating interplay of love and madness.

5. Milk and Blood, Love and Madness

We must believe that the divine architect built the uterus and the breasts with structures and mechanisms yet unknown, so that, by a constant law, the emptying of the uterus is followed by the production of milk [...]. Why then are the breasts affected by the uterus, and the other organs not, at least in the same way and with the same regularity? Certainly for that bond of sympathy, yet unknown in its mechanisms, that escapes anatomical investigation, but which one day may be completely clarified [...]. We must indeed admit that the harmony of the breasts with the uterus is a wonderful thing, but that it is yet unknown to human intelligence and anatomical investigation[22].

---

[22](Orig.) : « Si deve credere che il divino architetto abbia costruito l'utero e le mammelle con strutture e meccanismi ancora ignoti, di modo che, per una legge costante, allo svuotamento dell'utero fa seguito la produzione del latte [...]. Perché dunque le mammelle risentono delle influenze dell'utero, e non così gli altri organi, almeno nello stesso modo e con la stessa regolarità? Certamente per quel legame di simpatia, ancora sconosciuto nei

Puerperal insanity, a form of delirium found in pregnant, puerperal or suckling women, is a disturbance linked to the physiological function of maternity and – according to conjectures that were widely accepted, by Plato and Aristotle, and also in ecclesiastical circles – to the pathological essence of women, who were regarded in their most intimate nature as, by definition, inferior and *insane* creatures[23].

Official medicine in the nineteenth century, identifying a subtle link between women's physical and moral weakness, sought to demonstrate how «the female sex [is] subject to madness more than the male[...] due to the revolutions that take place in the weak and excitable female organism at the time of puberty, pregnancy, childbirth and suckling» Stoppato, cit. in Fiume, 1995: 105-106). The trauma of giving birth or losing milk, then, simply sets off a predisposition, a specific physiological condition of the woman in relation to madness[24]. Although modern medicine, fortunately, no longer allows itself such stigmatizing conjectures, any more than it believes that maternal milk is whitened blood, cooked in the kitchen of the woman's intestines[25], the etiology of puerperal psychosis is still uncertain and the link between milk and blood mysterious and inscrutable.

If we consider that during the suckling period the menstrual cycle is often interrupted, and certainly not because the fluid that had

---

suoi meccanismi, che sfugge all'indagine anatomica, ma che forse un giorno verrà completamente chiarito [...]. Bisogna infatti ammettere che l'armonia delle mammelle con l'utero è una cosa meravigliosa, ma che ancora è ignota all'intelligenza umana e all'indagine anatomica» (Ramazzini, 1703: 155-57).
[23] The Decretum Gratiani (1140), which became an official law of the Church in 1234 as an essential part of the Corpus Iuris Canonici, remaining in force until 1916, certified the physical inferiority and mental weakness of the woman: « « [...] virum ab Ambrosio appellatum non sexu, sed animi virtute; mulierem quoque nominat am sentiat non sexu corporis, sed mollicie mentis », (Causa XXXII, Quaestio 7, Caput XVIII).
(‹http://geschichte.digitale-sammlungen.de/decretum-gratiani/kapitel/dc _chapter_3_3362 ›, last access 5th March, 2013).
[24] Fiume offers examples and references on the question (1995: 83-117).
[25] Only in the second half of the twentieth century would the idea take shape that the link between uterus and breasts is not vascular but nervous, and that their absolute sympathy is due to the action of hormones, which are responsible for the development and shape of the breasts, as well as the production of milk.

nourished the child in the womb, ensuring its birth, had to change consistency and color to be able to continue its function outside of it and ensure the child's survival, then there seems nothing strange in the belief that the woman, in eliminating the blood, unconsciously wanted to repress her sexual impulses so as not to contaminate the milk and threaten the child with death[26].

If there were not this separation between milk and blood, or between mother and woman, the breast would be offered at the same time both to the man-lover and the child, with the effect of neither being able to distinguish between the desired woman and the forbidden mother. This subtle expression of the incest taboo is, however, unconsciously clear to the woman, who internalizes the ban and chooses to lose the milk or the blood, according to whether the maternal or the sexual instinct prevails in her. In this way suckling acts as a remedy for desire and female drives, a natural contraceptive and a barrier against excessive excitement, which could only be controlled in this way. The unconscious contradiction is therefore resolved by repression, and the conflict only apparently overcome (Freud, 1913). The good breast is therefore preferred to the bad one, and the providential aspect of milk-nutrition put before the blood of passion. But suckling becomes terrible for the wan mother who wears herself away in infinite suffering. Suckling is almost deadly for the woman who, *already ill*, drains herself in a vampire-like fusion with her child: the child is nourished by the mother and the mother by the child. She is consumed, happy to be emptied.

But often it is not the menstrual cycle that is interrupted, but the impetuous flow of milk. The loss of milk brings a trauma similar to that already mentioned, caused by weaning, in that it too echoes the primary pain of separation from the mother, not only by the child, but by what it represents when it depends totally on her: herself and her desire for self-preservation. The anguish of being abandoned and the fear of castration re-emerge in all their disturbing power and the mother thus becomes a dangerous prey to ravings that darken her mind. Milk and blood, excessive fluids by reason of their enigmatic and almost alchemical female nature, thus become disruptive signs of

---

[26] The regularization of the menstrual cycle after childbirth indicates the resumption of normal reproductive activity, and therefore of a possible new birth, which would compromise the survival of the child already born, to the extent that it would remove milk, nourishment and attention from it.

the woman's generative power, which make her silently responsible for life and death.

The ecstatic, orgiastic nature of the female risks turning into sudden madness, in ways as abrupt as they are paradoxical, and so the woman's body, in which the proximity of life and death is manifest in all its perturbing force is perceived as the source of abjection and disgust.

6. Biological Maternity and Cultural Maternity: Medea's Infanticide as a Social Product

Even if we want to interpret infanticide as the narcissistic need for self-preservation, or as the result of disharmony between sexual impulses and their consequences, sexuality and maternity must inevitably be regarded as experiences strictly defined by social factors too. Collective relations and customs have characterized maternity as not just a biological, but also a cultural, experience: being a mother, at least in Western patriarchal societies, has always been linked to the image of a married woman, and so to the presence of a husband, and thus the enactment of a cultural model has often been given priority over the biological event in itself.

Only after she had assumed the status of a married woman was Medea able to become a mother and generate children that guaranteed Jason the biological, social and sacral continuation of the οἶκος. Whatever the reasons for marital unhappiness, only the man had the prerogative to sever the bond. A lack of offspring allowed the husband to repudiate his wife (Lacey, 1968), while Medea would not have been able to, as she was wholly subject to the law of her husband, on whom her whole existence depended, and would never have been able to send her faithless husband away, or leave an unhappy marriage, to which death would have been preferable (Euripides, *Medea.* 243). For Jason, Medea has stained herself with the most serious faults against her family and the house of her father; she made Jason the center of her life, creating a blood tie with him by generating children for him. But Jason, who was everything for her, betrayed her trust and abandoned her bed, proving in this way to be «the most contemptible of men» (Euripides, *Medea.* 229). Medea faced the ἀγών μέγιστος courageously, wedding a man whose character and habits she did not know: she ran the risk, and she lost. And so, secure in the knowledge that she never failed in her role as devoted bride in any way, but united herself to Jason with solemn vows and provided him with heirs, Medea refuses to accept being deserted and decides to avenge the outrage she has suffered. «Touch [a woman's] right in marriage, and there's no bloodier spirit»[27], and, so, claiming her right to be a wife through her being a mother, Medea highlights the ends of the institution of the bond of wedlock – the children – and avenges herself through those children. Like «a lioness guarding her cubs» «she glares at [the servants]» «as soon as any of [them] goes near to her, or tries to speak» (vv. 187-189), and is just as capable of killing those children, if that means annihilating Jason and at the same time removing his means of revenge. An anguished woman, she becomes a terrifying mother when she refuses to passively accept discriminations in the οἶχοςε and castigates the person who has betrayed her, gripped by a terrible and disarming fury: killing her own children, she ensures that none of them will in turn avenge their father by turning on her.

Medea deliberately and consciously subordinates maternity to her desire for revenge, and prefers to be no longer a mother if she is repudiated as a bride. For Medea «not even maternity is an ineluctable destiny» (Beltrametti, 2000: 58), and, in her, being a woman no longer wholly coincides with being a mother. Even maternity is part of a network of cultural relations that change as the times change: and in Medea her image as a woman no longer coincides with mere fecund sexuality. The primeval mother that contains and transforms everything inside her, the Great Mother who gives life and takes it away, is embodied and repudiated in Medea, to the extent that she denies existence to children who are no longer only their father's, and rejects maternity as a purely biological fact if separated from the cultural bond of marriage.

Becoming a mother has a strictly social value for Medea that is tied to marriage, more than to the mere biological, natural fact. The scant importance patriarchal society attributes to this element, which forces biological maternity into the codified schemes of cultural maternity, defines infanticide as a rejection of the biological event, and not of the cultural one. The infanticides would not feel themselves to be «real mothers and therefore would not [feel] guilty towards a child» (Fiume, 1995: 115), if being a wife were the *sine qua non* for being able to become a mother, and being a mother were defined exclusively in the confines of being a wife. If Medea had not been the daughter of a king and the wife of a great commander, but an

---

[27] Euripides, *Medea* (265- 266), trans. Philip Vellacott.

illegitimate mother, a servant who had been seduced, or a concubine, alone and forgotten, her gesture would probably have had the same meaning, as it would have been dictated by the same sense of guilt for a painful and unhappy condition.

Only when these social and cultural pressures became less binding, thanks to strenuous battles against prevarications and prejudices, did the new mothers start going mad less often, and proved willing to bring up the children they had given birth to. In spite of this, although a woman's identity today is no longer defined exclusively in the marriage relation, and still less is female existence restricted to the sole function of maternity, there are more and more numerous and frequent cases of infanticide. This, however, is another subject. Infanticide, like maternity, is a moment of extreme importance for characterizing Medea as a tragic heroine and as a woman in particular: her maternal self re-echoes in all its poignant, devastating power, and makes her a figure who, despite the contingencies of her own time, acquires undoubtedly universal traits.

7. Θυμὸς and Βουλέυματα: Women Divided between Sexuality and Maternity

Medea's profound despair does not exclusively concern the dishonor she has received and the injustice she has suffered: being deprived of her husband and the erotic torment deriving from his absence make her extremely agitated and restless, essentially mad. The state of tension suffered by a woman who has been deprived of her bed – and not just in the sense of a vow of mutual faithfulness – risks becoming dangerous: deprived of sexual intercourse like rebellious virgins or scandalous wives, Medea acts in the grip of a frenzied fury that is almost madness. She lives to the full the painful torment that devastates her soul and transfigures her body: her face is transformed, her gaze becomes furious. Every wish is silenced in her, and she seems animated only by the desire for death. The profound link between sexuality and maternity is intimate and unfathomable in Medea; deprived of her bed, she also deprives herself of her children: perhaps, in the end, there was nothing else she could do.

A betrayed wife and a mother forced to perform a terrible choice, Medea experiences a conflict that is embodied in the celebrated monologue in the fifth episode (vv. 1019-80) for which the whole tragedy – a supreme example of Euripides' dramatic strategy – seems to have been simply a preparation. The decision-making process with which Medea prepares her vengeance and conceives the infanticide is an extraordinary example of self-analysis: lacerated by passion and reason, which, rather than clashing with each other, constantly intersect throughout the monologue and constitute her real inner tragedy[28], the heroine is presented in the contrasting drives that are generated inside her and in her divided self, which never finds rest or relief. Yet, her θυμός is not irrational, uncontrollable passion, but her intimate sensations, the inner capacity with which the human soul determines and directs its actions (Foley, 2001); capable both of devoting itself to pitiless plans for revenge and of falling back on the poignant love of a mother, the heart is stronger than intentions and is the cause of the greatest evils for men (Euripides, *Medea*. 1079-80). Medea's inner conflict, then, which develops in a constant, brilliant opposition between θυμός and βουλέυματα – between emotions and intentions – relates to the dichotomy between sexuality and maternity that we have already analyzed, and thus becomes a conflict between erotic desire and maternal love.

The complication and deterioration of the intimate tie that joins a woman's sexual sphere with her natural predisposition to generate children, is expressed in many representations of tragic heroines consumed by sick loves or ruined by incestuous unions. Women like Clytemnestra, Jocasta or Phaedra embody a sense of malaise towards children, whether natural or symbolic, caused by the breaking of a tie between sexuality and maternity that no longer cohabit in the bond of the nuptial pact; but it is with Medea and her total negation of maternity that we find the highest manifestation of this unease. Jason accuses her of sacrificing her children for the bed (Euripides, *Medea*. 1338), but Medea does not understand marriage as a pact of alliance and she repudiates herself as a mother, cursing her children: she kills them so that she may strike Jason to the heart, as he lives for those children and founds his power on them.

The power of blood and bodies, which constitutes the maternal tie, cannot, then, be denied in the name of social, public and symbolic values, on which the androcentric reality of the period was based. The tie felt and recognized by Medea is an authentic tie, made of living souls and bodies over which she claims a power of life and

---

[28] «And it is precisely this inseparable combination of rationality, passion and intelligence, in Medea's determination for revenge that makes it so very terrifying and, I think, far more tragic than a philosophical defeat of reason by passion» (Foley, 2001:257).

death in the name of the body that has generated them. In a society in which a woman changes only her master when she marries, passing from her father to the husband who exercises every form of power over her, Medea opposes the freedom of a woman who vindicates her maternal will and the force of a tie that cannot be bent to the grim law of honor and power.

CHAPTER TWO

Classical Myth and Folklore in *Beloved*

The demoniac figure of the witch of Colchis, who becomes a murderess because she cannot tolerate the demands of Greek society that she behave in a way alien to her nature, is soon isolated by insult and rejection, finding herself alone and insulted in her despair. Infanticide may be the most famous theme and the one most exploited in the myth, but the motif of the exclusion and removal of the barbarian Medea from Greek society is certainly another important semantic crux of the tragedy. Medea sums up in herself all those values connected with the free manifestation of individual personality, which much of Greek society at the time found it difficult to recognize, and so she was exorcized and cast out as a source of disorder. Euripides' criticism of fifth-century Athenian society, so concerned with trying to reach the unreachable that it had lost its humanity along the way[29], is in many respects similar to Toni Morrison's in her novel *Beloved*. Each work has its own techniques and aims, but both expose indifference in the face of a search for truths that challenge our standard assumptions, but are equally a part of the human spirit.

Euripides makes his criticism on three main fronts: he condemns the excesses of Sophist culture and the deliberately deceptive interpretation of reality with which it denies actual human values so as to continue to intellectually subjugate the weak; he rejects the false severity with which Greece claims to ensure fair justice, effectively denying the most fundamental human rights, thus ensuring a state

---

[29] The fault of the Athenians had been to aspire to the greatness of an absolute spiritual dimension, which was denied to man's frail reason. Having gone too far in its expansionist aims, Athens had denied the concrete value of the goals that man can achieve, and had alarmed Sparta, which in 431 BCE – the year of *Medea*'s first performance – invaded it, setting off the Peloponnesian War.

based on injustice and force; and he also blames the position of ethical and civil inferiority to which society relegated women. And yet it was women, despised and subjugated, who were able to contribute to renewing human relations and modifying the musty laws of a co-existence wholly lacking in intellectual interaction and founded on the logic of power. Only women could carry out this change, offering a profoundly human, alternative ethical model to the logic of war and the dynamics of power.

Euripides uses myth to show us the disintegration of the old civil and religious system of the πόλις and the overturning of many ancestral ethical values. Euripides had inherited the antilogies of the Sophists and delighted in displaying his expertise in handling arguments from two antithetical points of view, the witty stichomythies not only enlivening the rhythm and action, but dismantling certainties and values that were scarcely credible after the unhappy experience of the Peloponnesian War.

The overturning of patriarchal values echoes constantly in *Beloved* and the condemnation of indifference to the search for the truth is still more pitiless if this lack of interest becomes a collective, historical amnesia. Toni Morrison is close to, but also detached from, Euripides' mythical model and makes the subjugation of the weak – in this case physical as well as mental – the main theme of her novel. As a result the false pride of pluralist, liberal America is unmasked in the face of the horrors of slavery, which for too long denied the values of man, the dignity of the individual and respect for women.

Strikingly, Euripides uses the figure of a woman for an autobiographical digression on his condition as a writer and on the diversity of the intellectual in general (Paduano: 1968: chap. 2). Dramatically overturning the categories of sex and race, he makes a barbarian woman his mouthpiece as an intellectual who has not been corrupted by the cultural mystifications and advantages of power, and so is punished with moral exile for her attempt to return Athenian civilization to more authentic cultural models. All this is reflected in Morrison and her opposition to the West's cultural hegemony. A woman and a writer of Afro-American descent, she exposes the violence perpetrated on black skins and female bodies, and, blending classical myth with African folklore, denounces the cultural arrogance with which Europe has always suffocated the voices of the weak.

It would therefore have been a contradiction in terms, as well as extremely implausible, to turn the theme of one of the strongest and most popular myths in the Western tradition into a whole novel. Not wanting to take Euripides' version as an authentic model, Morrison preferred to keep just the memory of the myth of Medea and, with great power, to run Afro-American history alongside it. In this way, traces of Medea can be found in Morrison's literary territory, with latent references and probable analogies, overturning the classical model and the misuse of power in a wholly female masterpiece.

1. Afro-American Reception of the Classics: Bernal and the «Classica Africana»

Martin Bernal's controverisal *Black Athena* (1987) sparked off a lively intellectual debate on the centrality of African culture in determining Western identity. This huge work, conceived in four parts, of which so far only the first two volumes have been published, set out to demonstrate, with somewhat weak and less than rigorous philological and etymological methods, the Afro-Asiatic roots of classical civilization, and hence of Western culture in general. Claiming that classical Greek culture was significantly influenced by Phoenician and ancient Egyptian civilization, he claimed to demonstrate how these ties have been deliberately disregarded in the modern age for racist reasons[30].

> The essential force behind the rejection of the tradition of massive Phoenician influence on early Greece was the rise of racial – as opposed to religious – anti-semitism. This was because Phoenicians were correctly perceived to have been culturally very close to the Jews. (Bernal 1987: 2)

According to Bernal, it was during the period of Europeanization, particularly in the nineteenth century, that white authors began to identify the classics with the dominant, hegemonic – and Eurocentric – culture of power and racial discrimination. The presence of a vital, Afro-Asian contribution to the origins of Greek civilization, which

---

[30] It is unnecessary to recall that the concept of race and the natural superiority of some races over others is a post-Columbus construction. Recent studies have shown how the ancient Greeks and Romans had no prejudices linked to skin color – although they were in contact with dark-skinned populations – (Snowden, 1970, 1983), but based the legitimacy of slavery on other factors just as pernicious, such as the intellectual inferiority that Aristotle himself saw as inherent in some ethnic groups, which were consequently inevitably destined to be subjected.

later became European and now North-Atlantic civilization, subject to a process of globalization, was therefore deliberately repressed with the invention of the ancient «Greek miracle». The supposed Greek miracle had the great function of providing the foundations for the illusion of a European cultural superiority that redeemed the history of European civilization of any debt towards older ones.

Giving Greece rather than Africa the honor of having partly determined the birth of Western civilization, white intellectuals had simply, and quite deliberately, denied connections and links that otherwise might have prevented modern Europe from looking at the past – and at Athens in particular – through an ideological prism of race, and so justifying the noble character of a society based on slavery. Europe's heavy cultural debt to the ancient Near East, which can be summarized in the motto *ex oriente lux*, is no longer a secret, any more than the improper use the West made of the classics to prop up racism and promote Eurocentrism against the East and the black continent; it is incontestable that many European classicists in the eighteenth and nineteenth centuries used the classics in a racist manner to promote a Eurocentric vision of the world in a Europe that was becoming more and more intolerant (Bernal, 1987: 1-73).

In opposition to the prevailing, essentially Eurocentric vision, Bernal's Afrocentrism offers to exalt Africa's historical, cultural role in the history of civilizations, and its specific contribution to the genesis of the West. Afrocentrism, then, in the sense of the affirmation of all the various aspects of black identity is simply a contra-hegemonic perspective to bring to the cultural tyranny of the West, equally atavistic and a mirror image of it. As van Binsbergen suggests (2004: 104), in giving intellectuals outside the predominant, North-Atlantic political and cultural circle and the white tradition, a historic, independent and even older birthright that allows them to operate legitimately under the sun of intellectual globalization, Bernal had quite simply made a revolutionary contribution to global knowledge policies in our age, tackling central themes of our time, such as the struggle of minorities to affirm their identity, post-colonial theory, multiculturalism, and the discovery of the hegemonic nature of North-Atlantic knowledge systems.

In 1992, in the course of the debate following publication of *Black Athena*, the classicist and philologist Mary Lefkowitz published an article entitled «Not Out of Africa: The Origins of Greece and the Illusions of the Afrocentrists», in which Afrocentrism is presented as a non-academic and often false need of American blacks to situate themselves in a tradition. She writes:

> It was inevitable, therefore, that the black peoples in the English-speaking countries of this continent, as they developed a sense of their own identity, would want to show that they had a stake in the cultural legacy of Greece. (Lefkowitz, 1992: 31)

Bernal's ideas were further refuted in *Black Athena Revisited*, written in collaboration with her colleague Guy MacLean Rogers in 1996. For Lefkowitz, the Afrocentric tendency is only a monolithic attempt – no less dangerous than the Eurocentric one – to re-read history so as to fill up a worrying void in the present. In the same year Michele Valerie Ronnick responded to the so-called «Black Athena debate» with a calm invitation to look beyond the Bernal-Lefkowitz dispute and officially presented «Classica Africana» as a specialization in classical studies. Imitating the title of Meyer Reinhold's pioneering book *Classica Americana*, Ronnick used the expression «Classica Africana» for the first time to indicate a new field of classical studies that would become part of American academic orthodoxy:

> It is a time for scholars and educators to look beyond the Martin Bernal-Mary Lefkowitz debate, and turn toward other types of research. One of these new approaches is Classica Africana, a name patterned upon Meyer Reinhold's pioneering book, Classica Americana (Detroit: Wayne State University Press, 1984), which examined the impact of classics upon eighteenth and nineteenth-century America. The new subfield sharpens the wide view taken by Reinhold concerning the influence of the Greco-Roman heritage in America, and looks at the undeniable impact, both positive and negative, that this heritage has had upon people of African descent, not only in America but also in the Western World. The past 400-500 years offer us many noteworthy examples of people of African descent who used their knowledge of classical studies in their creative and/or professional lives. This

terra incognita of intellectual inquiry is worthy of attention today and tomorrow.[31]

Before the publication of «Black Athena» and the polemic that
followed, the study of black classicism in America had been wholly
in the hands of the black intellectual community, while today classicists use the expression «Classica Africana» to define and recognize
the Afro-American cultural and literary tradition, as well as the contribution it makes with this or that classic to the Western canon. It
would, in any case, be unthinkable to imagine the two traditions as
completely separate one from the other, or without any mutual
influence and cross-fertilization. The Afro-American presence merg-
es with the Native American one, as it does with that of immigrants,
in a wonderfully intricate tangle of voices and colors: there is not just
one canon in American literature; on the contrary, it bears the sign of
numerous, extremely different presences that make it up, both when
it admits them to its pages, and when it labors to forget them[32].
American literature is not the literature of the canon, as, in the multiplicity of canons that represent America's linguistic and cultural
multiplicity, the very idea of a canon, with its claim to cohesion and
oneness, collapses.

The areas of interest in this new research field of classical studies
included, above all, the study of works with which Afro-American
classicists past and present had contributed to the creation of a classical tradition in America: *in primis*, those of William Sanders Scarborough, «the first member of his race to prepare a Greek text-book
suitable for university use» (Ronnick, eds., 2005: 6)[33]. There followed

---

[31] Ronnick, M.V., (1997) «After Bernal and Mary Lefkowitz: Research Opportunities in Classica Africana». *Negro History Bullettin 60*: 1-12;
(http://department.monm.edu/Classics/cpl/PromotionalMaterials/African
a.htm, last access 5th March, 2013).

[32] See Toni Morrison, *Playing in the Dark*, 1990.

[33] This was an extremely valuable contribution by Ronnick to «Classica
Africana», publishing the autobiography of the first classicist of African
descent, whose genius triumphed over injustice and adversity.
« Notwithstanding the passage of years between Scarborough's lifetime and
our own, it is deeply shaming for classicists to read of a 'colleague' excluded
on grounds of his race from hotels that were meant to be hosting the dele-
gates of academic conferences at which he had been invited to speak, never
being able to rely on a constant salary even when in possession of a tenured
chair at Wilberforce, denied a pension after forty-three years of service to

the study of the presence of blacks in antiquity and how they were perceived by the ancient Greeks and Romans; and, finally, the different ways in which Afro-American writers have adapted myths.

Although, from Michele Valerie Ronnick to Christa Buschendorf, from Jacqueline de Weever to Shelley Haley, there have been many studies of the links between the classics and Afro-American literature, very little has been written on the ways in which Afro-American writers have adapted and reworked classical myths; still less on the influence of the Greek-Roman tradition on Afro-American female writers, many of whom have incorporated themes, archetypes and typical figures of Western narrative discourse in their works.

The first volume to be centered exclusively on re-workings of classical myths by Afro-American writers was *Ulysses in Black: Ralph Ellison, Classicism, and African American Literature*, written by Patrice D. Rankine in 2006. *Crossroads in the Black Aegean: Oedipus, Antigone, and Dramas of the African Diaspora* by Barbara Goff and Michael Simpson appeared the following year. In it, the tragedy of Oedipus and Antigone, prominent figures in the Theban trilogy, are assimilated to works of the African diaspora to translate crucial themes in the post-colonial context, such as identity, the imposition of civilization on barbarians, and cultural transmission.

The reasons that have determined this long silence have probably also included, as Rankine herself claims, the refusal by part of a fringe of Afro-American academics, to give the same critical treatment to texts influenced by the classics as to those that respond perfectly to the Black Aesthetic «Black classicism negatively affects the reception of the works of black authors,» writes Rankine (2006: 19), and for this reason many works containing references to the classics, notes Tracy Walters, are often not as successful, or simply as well received by critics, as they should have been.

> [...] because some African Americanists dismiss the western classics as Eurocentric and antithetical to a Black literary tradition – or Black aesthetic - those texts reflecting a classical influence are not granted the same critical analysis reserved for non-classically inspired works. (Walters, 2007: 5)

---

the profession, and having to rely upon rare ingenuity to get access to the publications that he needed for his research» (Greenwood, 2009: 92).

Yet, according to Rankine, this rejection of everything in any way steeped in classicism is accompanied by a mirror attitude in which the incorporation of the classics seems, on the contrary, to be an integral part of black cultural identity itself (Rankine, 2006: 37-43). Although European cultural hegemony determined a radical reaction against the classics, the contra-hegemonic discourse with which a significant part of Attic tragedy opposed power on many fronts, has meant that Greek-Roman literature has also attracted a great deal of attention from Afro-American writers.

Black classicism, then, a conscious component of the Afro-American cultural and literary identity, is to be understood in the light of a shared attitude of resistance to power. Opposition to a religious system in which man is the victim of capricious, envious gods, and the rejection of an autocratic regime or even a democracy that is so unjust as to deny the humanity of a foreign woman, bring Greek tragedy close to that of those on the threshold of the twentieth century who still had to face the injustices of slavery.

Resistance to divine power is frequent in Aeschylus or Sophocles, just like the later resistance to political power in Euripides, and it expresses opposition to a still more terrible power – that of whites over blacks, men over women – as well as the adaptability and polysemy of myth, which lends itself to endless interpretations.

2. A Female Version of the Myth: Toward a New Black Aesthetic

In 2007, with *African American Literature and the Classicist Tradition*, Tracy L. Walters restricted her field of enquiry to the rewriting of myths by women, and in particular those myths centered on the theme of maternity, which had been widely used in Afro-American literature. Walters's study is an extremely important contribution to the study of female reception of the classics, and classical mythology in particular. In it, she recognizes the approach of Afro-American women writers to the classics as that of double minorities, to the extent that race and gender have determined a double exclusion in them similar to that described by Liz Lochhead in Scotland.

> For African American women writers in particular, the Persephone figure serves as an archetype for Black women who by virtue of their race and gender see themselves

as double minorities oppressed by patriarchy. (Walters, 2007: 27)

During the twentieth and twenty-first centuries Afro-American women writers have gone back to classical myth, using a perspective that is not just black but specifically female. «Like many other women [...] Morrison's goal is to present classical myth from the Black female perspective,» writes Walters (2007: 114). Overturning the racist, sexist, androcentric and hegemonic models of some of the classical myths, they incorporate a new mythological tradition in their narrative, with its roots in Afro-American experience and at last includes every aspect of the black female subject. The lives of blacks are told for the first time through the eyes of blacks, and, what is more, from an entirely female perspective.

The mythical figures of inferiors offended, betrayed and imprisoned, or of strong women who seek and find deliverance, changing from victims to executioners, are those who lend themselves best to this kind of rewriting, like those linked to the theme of maternity in general. And so mythological figures like Demeter, Persephone, Niobe or Medea are transformed into dark-skinned mothers who live out the drama of separation from their children or become murderesses by necessity. Important female tropes, such as incest, oppression and sexual violence, the relation between mothers and daughters, or the struggle to affirm one's identity, became focal points in Toni Morrison's rewriting, and in the work of Afro-American women writers in general, as, given that these topics were genuine taboos in the black community itself, they were hidden truths to be revealed. In this way, the particular experience of Afro-American women was linked to that of mythical mothers in an eternal, timeless tie that confirmed the universal approach of the writing, and at last offered these women the possibility of giving voice to those who for too long had been forced into silence or were unable to speak.

The complex and incessant task for Afro-American women writers of rewriting myths was begun by Phillis Wheatley. In 1773 she published her first and only collection of poetry, entitled *Poems on Various Subjects, Religious and Moral*; since then, the reworking of the classics, and of myths in particular, continues to be tinged, for American women writers of African descent, with many colors that, in their thousands of overtones and tonalities, help repaint the original wonderfully afresh each time.

During the eighteenth and nineteenth centuries blacks had appropriated classical myths, substantially to demonstrate their humanity in the eyes of their white masters. The use of white tradition was seen as a challenge with which to demonstrate not only the validity and respectability of black poetic genius (*pace* Thomas Jefferson, who had described Phillis Wheatley's poetry as poor and elementary, inferior to white poetry in form and content), but also to lay claim to equal dignity and equal right to be admitted to the category of human beings. The resulting surprise and satisfaction are palpable in the words of William Sanders Scarborough:

> I was on my program for my paper on «The Chronological Order of Plato's Works», designing to prove the order in point of time of Plato's writings by the Greek used by him and by the circumstances that surrounded him at the time of writing. The [session] was held in the Rotunda of the University used as its library. The white aristocracy turned out in large numbers. There was hardly standing room. [...] The feeling that came over me was a strange one, as I stepped forward to present my paper. Every eye was fixed upon me and a peculiar hush seemed to pervade the room. It was a rare moment. Like a flash the past unrolled before my mind, my early Atlanta examinations, Calhoun's famous challenge, that no Negro could learn Greek. For a moment I felt embarrassed as I faced my audience aware too that they must experience a peculiar feeling at the situation – a Negro member of that learned body standing in intellectual manhood among equals and where no Negro had never been allowed to enter, save as a servant – a Negro to discuss the writings of a Greek philosopher. (Scarborough cit. in Ronnick, eds., 2005: 121)

In this way many Afro-American women began to study the classics and rewrite myths to affirm not only the right and dignity of an existence, but also the power and force of their sex and race[34]. But in the 1940s and 1950s, rather than needing to demonstrate their hu-

---

[34] See, for example, *A Voice from the South* (1892) by Anna Julia Cooper, in which the marginalization of women is contrasted with the freedom and respect given to female poets and writers in ancient Greece.

manity or equal intellectual dignity, they rejected the a-historical universality of Greek-Roman myth in favor of Afro-American folklore and the mythological tradition of the old black continent.

> By and large the Black novelists of the fifties rejected the a-historical universality of Greco-Roman myth and ritual for a mixture of Christian and social myths and rituals rooted in the particularity of the Black American experience. For example, the myth of White supremacy and the rituals that reinforce and perpetuate the Manichean Black and White, evil and good, significations of Western mythology with its overtones of an apocalyptic clash are still major sources for themes, symbols, and images in the novels of the fifties. (Bell, cit. in Walters, 2007: 10)

This change of direction in reworking myths, which meant that Afro-American writers in the 1950s found themselves reconsidering the social and religious myths of Africa and distancing themselves more and more from Western models, would lead in the following decades to the rise of the «Black Arts Movement». Basing themselves on the political theories of black nationalism (Black Power) and supporting the Civil Rights Movement (1955-1968), the artists belonging to this movement sought to create a new form of popular, political art. Attacking all the values of the white middle classes and rejecting Western poetic conventions, they aimed to produce an art that would be significant for people of color, able to promote the idea of black separatism[35].

In this scenario, Toni Morrison with her innovative black aesthetic takes her place midway between tradition and innovation, classicism and modernism, Greece and Africa: recognizing the importance of drawing on every culture to describe the universal features of human experience, she turns equally to the models of the classical tradition and African folklore, imbuing her narrative with both traditions, and mixing Greek and African mythologies to bring out com-

---

[35] One of the most immediate and visible consequences of this movement was certainly the creation from the early 1970s onwards of many university departments for the study of Afro-American literature and culture. In this context we can see the importance of the sub-field of «Classica Africana» as the first opportunity for Afro-American writers to discuss these questions.

mon human features and, at the same time, explore the universal character of the myth.

Unlike Eurocentric and Afrocentric criticism, which recognizes the enormous difficulties in establishing a link between the Greek-Roman and African traditions, Morrison insists on the affinities between the two cultures and on the literary heritage of myth. Approaching the classical tradition does not necessarily mean having to sacrifice the black voice: on the contrary, as she demonstrates, both can coexist within the same narrative: constructed in this way, it retrieves Western myth and at the same time is rooted in black experience.

3. Toni Morrison and the Classics: Mythology and Folklore

Morrison's interest in mythology was clear from her adolescent years, growing up amid oral storytelling that the old shared in the community.

> There were two kinds of education going on: one was the education in the schools which was print-oriented; and right side by side with it was this other way of looking at the world that was not only different than what we learned about in school, it was coming through another sense. People told stories. (Neustadt, 1980 in Taylor-Guthrie, eds., 1994: 90)[36]

After four years of Latin at Lorain High School, Morrison continued her studies of classical literature at Harvard from 1951 to 1953, which culminated in 1955 with a thesis entitled *Virginia Woolf's and William Faulkner's Treatment of the Alienated*. Already in this first work she was probably influenced by its being a «minor classic», as she herself says in an interview of 1981 (LeClair, 1981 in Taylor-Guthrie, eds., 1994:125) and in another of 1985 (Jones and Vinson, in Taylor-Guthrie, eds., 1994: 176). In it, there emerges the tragic

---

[36] The official nature of learning is described alongside the informality of acquisition; Morrison brings out her the sharp dissonance between the culture of books and that of voices, between what was taught in the schools and what was spontaneously acquired thanks to the oral storytelling of the community. This opposition relates to the dichotomy between orality and writing, as well as between standard speech and dialect in Liz Lochhead.

mode of her writing, to the extent that, including processes of revelation and catharsis, she identifies all the elements of classical tragedy in Faulkner's work and introduces the sense of the tragic that was to pervade her whole future output. In *Unspeakable Things Unspoken*, a lesson held at Michigan University on October 7, 1988, she claimed:

> A large part of the satisfaction I have always received from reading Greek tragedy, for example, is in its similarities to Afro-American communal structures […] and African religion and philosophy. In other words, that is part of the reason it has quality for me – I feel intellectually at home there. But that could hardly be so for those unfamiliar with my «home«, and hardly a requisite for the pleasure they take. (Morrison, 1989: 2-3)

The relation with the classics, however, does not subsume hierarchical ties of superiority and subordination:

> […] (Greek tragedy) makes available these varieties of provocative love because it is masterly – not because the civilization that is its referent was flawless or superior to all others. […] Finding or imposing Western influences in/on Afro-American literature has value, but when its sole purpose is to place value only where that influence is located it is pernicious. (ibid.: 3, 10)

On the contrary, the constant interconnections between Greek and African culture serve to reveal what has been hidden by the dominant culture over the centuries.

> In engaging Greece and Rome the author is not borrowing from or even insisting on her right to share in a pure, white legacy. Instead, […] she is re-appropriating a tradition which emerged from interactions and affinities between Europe and Africa, and thus was never either pure or white. (Roynon, 2007: 5)

Using various strategies to transform the classical tradition as well as American culture, Morrison re-reads history and re-tells the past from a new perspective. The frequent use of classical paradigms, however, is not designed to celebrate an ancient past that has few affinities with the African tradition, but to subvert the very models adopted and, through them, some aspects of the dominant American culture. In this perspective it is understandable that the use of archetypes is not just designed to re-tell the histories of the conquered, but to criticize the conventional ideology of the victors. Thus, the paradigm of the tragic hero, divided between desire and necessity, and ironically condemned in the freedom of his choice to submit to the consequences of an ill-starred fate, becomes, for example, a tool for contesting the acritical acceptance of the prevailing culture and the unconditional celebration of the very idea of freedom. «E' un paese libero, quest uomo è mio»[37] was how Alessandro Portelli entitled one of the sections of *Canoni Americani* (Portelli, 2004: 12), to indicate the incoherent absurdity of this contradiction, in the name of which America had justified slavery during the eighteenth century. «For southern gentlemen the possession of slaves was not just incidental, but, implicitly, a constituent part of their pride as free men,» continues Portelli (ivi)[38], confirming the oxymoronic, almost schizophrenic nature of a claim that contains many features of one of the most widespread American ideas of freedom: that by which freedom does not concern the relations between individuals in a society, but the mere desire of the individual who demands the right to act without any restraints being placed on his range of choice. But this is a poor kind of freedom, if governed by arrogance, and a limited one too – more so than the limitations that are imposed on the freedom of others. Portelli continues:

> It is a solitary, absolute freedom, which recognizes [...] no limitation and no criterion of reciprocity. [...] it is the solipsistic freedom of the frontier [...] or of international relations in which the United States does not always manage to recognize the sovereignty of others unless as an impediment to its own. [...] A free country in short can designate both a country in which people are free, and also a country that is free in the world to do what it wants «without bothering about borders».[39]

---

[37] Trans. « It is a free country, this man is mine».

[38] «Il possesso di schiavi non era solo incidentale per i gentiluomini del Sud, ma implicitamente costitutivo del proprio orgoglio di uomini liberi».

[39] (Orig.): E' una libertà solitaria e assoluta, che non conosce [...] nessun limite e nessun criterio di reciprocità. [...] è la libertà solipsistica della

Equally obnoxious to Morrison is the attitude of many present-day white writers towards literature, almost as if they were its only undisputed «proprietors»:

> Contemporary writers deliberately exclude from their conscious writerly world the subjective appraisal of groups perceived as «other» [...]. It only seems that the canon of American literature is «naturally» or «inevitably» white. (Morrison, 1989: 13-14)

In a cultural context structured in this way, made up of separatisms and divisions of power, the choice of writing an almost choral novel in which the community's voice has a decisive role is unusual, to say the least, and certainly provocative. Adopting the Greek chorus, which brings classical tragedy so close to Afro-American community structures in its constant opposition between individual will and the collective good, and because it translates «the heroic struggle between the claims of community and individual hubris» (Morrison, 1998: 125), has the aim of criticizing rampant individualism and the difficulty of interpersonal relations in the America of today.

Autonomy is freedom and translates into the much championed and revered «individualism»; newness translates into «innocence»; distinctiveness becomes difference and the erection of strategies for maintaining it; authority and absolute power become a romantic, conquering «heroism», virility, and the problematics of wielding absolute power over the lives of others. All the rest are made possible by this last, it would seem – absolute power called forth and played against and within a natural and mental landscape conceived of as a «raw, half-savage world» (Morrison, 1992: 44-45).

Morrison continues:

> There is something about the Greek chorus, for example, that reminds me of what goes on in Black churches and in jazz where there are two things. You have a response, obviously. The chorus being the community who partici-

---

frontiera [...] o quella di relazioni internazionali in cui gli Stati Uniti non sempre riescono a riconoscere la sovranità altrui se non come impedimento alla propria. [...] *A free country* insomma può designare sia un paese in cui le persone sono libere, sia anche un paese che è libero nel mondo di fare quello che vuole «senza badare alle linee di confine».

> pates in this behavior and is shocked by it or horrified by it or they like or they support it. Everybody is in it. And it has something also with the way in which those stories are told because the reader becomes a participant in the books, and I have to make it possible for the reader to respond the way I would like the chorus to in addition to the choral effects in the book itself (Jones-Vinson, 1985, in Taylor-Guthrie, eds., 1994: 176).

Her decision to construct a polyphonic novel, then, was not just due to the presence of a community observing and commenting on the events, but by the novel's invitation to directly involve the reader, who «as part of the population of the text, is implicated» (Morrison, 1989: 22).

> Being in church and knowing that the function of the preacher is to make you get up, you do say yes, and you do respond back and forth. The music is unplanned and obviously not structured, but something is supposed to happen, so the listener participates. (Ruas, 1981 in Taylor-Guthrie, eds., 1994: 101)

This is possible only if the story being told is understood no longer as the property of the person telling it, but as belonging to the whole community, which, as it draws on the collective patrimony, is constantly transforming and recreating it. The specific cultural patrimony, however, is not the only custodian of archetypal models, which recur in the most distant and different cultures, and survive over the centuries, demanding the most various interpretations. All sorts of archetypal themes are recognizable by the whole human race, since the contents of the collective unconscious refer back to the historical-cultural patrimony of the whole of humanity.

> [...] And even when we were sitting around telling stories, the stories were never the property of the teller. They were community property or they were family property and anybody could elaborate on them or change them and retell them. You heard them over and over again. (Jones-Vinson, 1985, in Taylor-Guthrie, eds., 1994: 176)-

They were not just inherited tales, but inherited possibilities of tales. Re-using traditional elements, often playfully and subversively, allowed them to confirm the universal character of myth and to re-form the conventional dynamics of gender and race – as well as the disparity between national aspirations and the existing socio-political reality. The proud conviction by which the classics are the exclusive domain of a restricted group of white authors was thus ambushed and sabotaged by means of the classics themselves. Morrison does not write for whites, but for those with a dark skin:

> We have always been imagining ourselves. [...] We are the subjects of our own narrative, witnesses to and participants in our own perspective, and, in no way coincidentally, in the experience of those with whom we have come in contact. (Morrison, 1989: 9)

This use of classical motifs might, on the one hand, confirm the impossibility of a black text existing outside the white tradition, outside the Western canon; at the same time, the subversion of Western mythology might also translate its inadequacy in representing black identity: on the other hand, the construction of identity and, with it, black literature, from the inside and autonomously, without external super-structures or conditioning, has always been difficult and demanding. But fortune favors the bold, and, rather than hastily dismissing classical mythology as hegemonic and dictatorial, Morrison exploits and challenges it, examining its possibilities for her purposes.

4. Myth and History

The role of classical myth in validating and then celebrating the European conquest of the New World is examined in Love (2003) through the myth of Kore, which underlies all the acts of sexual violence that pervade the whole novel. Here, in fact, sexual violence is assimilated to American colonialism, and exposed as an expression of imperialistic power. The motif of sexual violence, extremely frequent in Greek mythology, is also present in The Bluest Eye (1970), where, as de Weever notes (1991), the mythic proportions of Demeter's and Persephone's experience is scaled down to the dimensions of everyday urban life, and the mythical motif of death and rebirth completely altered and inverted[40].

Although there are clear traces of Greek myth in her novels, the narrative is always profoundly rooted in Afro-American folklore; and so, if the Western reader easily recognizes the myth of Icarus in Song of Solomon (1977), for Toni Morrison the motif of flight is a specific reference to the capacity of blacks to fly.

> The flying myth in Song of Solomon. If it means Icarus to some readers, fine; I want to take credit for that. But my meaning is specific: it is about black people who could fly. That was always part of the folklore of my life; flying was one of our gifts. (LeClair, 1981, in Taylor-Guthrie, eds., 1994: 122)

The cultural myth at times overshadows and surpasses the classical one, but then, suddenly, the two come together again. This is what happens in Beloved, whose fidelity to Afro-American mythology blends with classical Western myth, and Morrison's revisionism reaches its acme.

> «Dusting off the myth», as [Toni Morrison] likes to put it, examines and develops the tensions between Western and other myths to analyze the contradictory reality of American society. The relations of intertextuality and intratextuality between myths are a pretext for narrative experimentation. [...] The narrative discourse takes off from the inevitable conflict caused by the collision of the mythic ambition with the often oppressive reality in which the characters flounder as they try to give a sense to their lives. (Scarpa, 1994: 70)

Tragedy and classical myth, like some Afro-American cultural top-oi, are re-used to subvert the canonical representations of slavery and cancel the widespread conception of the so-called «Lost Cause» as a defeat best forgotten[41]. Criticism of Western mythology, however,

---

[40] In the hobbling walk of Pecola Breedlove and its connection with incest we can glimpse the myth of Oedipus.

[41] «The Lost Cause is an interpretation of the American Civil War (1861–1865) that seeks to present the war, from the perspective of Confederates,

goes hand in hand with that of African folklore, which is understandably privileged in the course of the novel for obvious reasons of personal genesis and cultural memory, but is never spared if, as effectively happens, collective amnesia strikes not only the whites but the blacks too, and a sense of guilt prevents Sethe, as much as anyone else, from remembering her past.

«Rememory» and «disremember» are two fundamental neologisms in the text and translate, respectively, the collective memory and the difficulty of remembering. The former is used in the text both as a noun and a verb and translates the need to remember a remote past, while the latter, as Franca Cavagnoli notes (*Postfazione* to *Amatissima*, 1996: 387-391), is vernacular in origin, suggesting both *remember* and *dismember*, and contains both the negation of memory (dis-remember) and the physical suffering produced by the act of remembering. It is a painful process for those who have lost their identity and either do not want to, or cannot, remember. The dismembering of the body that has been mangled by the memory thus refers to the ritual violence perpetrated on the blacks, the mangled bodies of the slaves, and the chokecherry tree cut into Sethe's back by the whip; but it could equally be a further reference to classical mythology and the dismembering of male victims in matriarchal societies.

Without concessions, Morrison unflinchingly lays bare the complexities of the social and human dynamics in which the oppressed have appropriated the values of the oppressors, becoming accomplices in abdicating from discussing the real causes of every problem.

---

in the best possible terms. Developed by white Southerners, many of them former Confederate generals, in a postwar climate of economic, racial, and gender uncertainty, the Lost Cause created and romanticized the 'Old South' and the Confederate war effort, often distorting history in the process. For this reason, many historians have labeled the Lost Cause a myth or a legend. It is certainly an important example of public memory, one in which nostalgia for the Confederate past is accompanied by a collective forgetting of the horrors of slavery. Providing a sense of relief to white Southerners who feared being dishonored by defeat, the Lost Cause was largely accepted in the years following the war by white Americans who found it to be a useful tool in reconciling North and South. The Lost Cause has lost much of its academic support but continues to be an important part of how the Civil War is commemorated in the South and remembered in American popular culture», Encyclopedia Virginia «http://www. encyclopediavirginia.org/Lost_Cause_The», last access 12th March, 2013).

It is a profound analysis of the negative sides of the Afro-American psyche, whose epic proportions – seen, for example, in the extraordinary capacity of black women to give life in death – celebrate a race of survivors, determined to maintain their human identity at all costs.

Morrison's novel is based on a news item from 1855, which she chanced upon while editing *The Black Book*[42]. The article reported the case of Margaret Garner, a runaway slave from Kentucky, who was being hunted down by a posse who, as laid down by the 1851 law on runaways, would make her captive again. She slit her daughter's throat to save her from the horrors of slavery. In *Modern Medea: A Family Story of Slavery and Child-Murder from the Old South*, (1998) Steven Weisenburger gives an account of the whole story, which has various analogies with the episode of the myth of Medea as told by Euripides and Seneca. Transposing the action from ancient Corinth to nineteenth-century America, then, is not so much a process of literary creation, as an interpretation that has historical confirmation, and that is translated in the novel into the shifting time perspective of the action, which differentiates it from the tragedies of Euripides and Seneca.

As Morrison tells the story, in fact, it starts after the infanticide, presenting the character of Sethe from a later perspective than the character of Medea in the Greek drama. Although both Euripides (vv. 37-43) and Seneca (vv. 380-96) anticipate the epilogue of the tragedy in the words of the nurse, the infanticide is the inevitable conclusion of the dramatic action. In *Beloved*, by contrast, the infanticide re-emerges from the memories of the various characters and takes on the contours of a tortuous process of redemption, in the course of which Sethe has to come to terms with a past that she is trying in vain to forget: «To Sethe, the future was a matter of keeping the past at bay. The 'better life' she believed she and Denver were living was simply not that other one» (*Beloved*: 42).

One of the metaphors in the novel is the achieving of self-consciousness by a people that anonymously brought about the genesis of a culture – America's – that was born out of violence and that hides itself in violence. Morrison's great challenge is not only that of seeking to revive the history of the oppressed through the language

---

[42] This is a collection of documents on 300 years of Afro-American life, detailing not just the living conditions of the black community, but also many examples of Afro-American culture, from photographs to bills of sale, from newspaper cuttings to examples of poetry.

of the oppressors, but to make the oppressed aware that their role in forming Western culture and literature was far from marginal.

> Afro-American culture exists, and though it is clear (and becoming clearer) how it has responded to Western culture, the instances where and the means by which it has shaped Western culture are poorly recognized or understood. I want to address the ways in which the presence of Afro-American literature and the awareness of its culture both resuscitate the study of literature in the United States and raise that study's standards. (Morrison, 1989: 3)

In this scenario, the invention of a matrilineal genealogy, as in all her novels, and the centrality of female characters sharply divided by generation into children, mothers, adults and the old, make the novel a kind of saga in which individual identity cannot disregard collective identity, which is the only guarantee of survival for American blacks in the predatory society of the United States.

5. Redirecting Infanticide

The myth of Medea, which the novel clearly has in mind, is overturned in the figure of Sethe, her maternal love and her brazen resistance to power: and, for the first time, the hubris of a tragic character is no longer presented as a fault, but as a virtue. By subverting the stereotype of the black matriarch from which she derives, Sethe can embody the archetype of the mother who gives her life with infinite generosity and defends it from any threat, and yet who can take it back with the same speed with which she gave it. The gesture of defiance with which she cuts her daughter's throat to save her from slavery gives her a certain austerity, like Medea in being fully aware of what she is doing, but, unlike her, in being driven. not by pride or vengeance, but by a spirit of freedom and by her inability to contemplate separation from her daughter.

As in Euripides, so in Seneca, Medea is presented as a woman split between passion and reason, and therefore torn between her desire for vengeance and maternal love. Yet, while the semantic keystone of Euripides' play is Medea's awareness of being profoundly divided, Seneca focuses on the more irrational side of the heroine, the *furor* that seems to guide every thought and determine every action. The laceration of Medea's soul, which emerges in the celebrated monologue in the fifth episode, and above all in the last lines of Euripides' play, is an extremely modern example of the character's capacity for self-analysis; yet, as we have already mentioned, Medea's θυμός does not indicate the irrationality of her passion, but rather the passion, gusto and will that direct her action – whether toward good or evil.

Instead of Medea's inner conflict, Toni Morrison presents the cool lucidity with which Sethe decides to kill Beloved, and instead of the motif of infanticide as a conscious act of revenge that emerges from a difficult, but free and individual choice, she shows us the immediacy of an instinctive and only apparently unnatural gesture, which channels the reader's compassion onto the protagonist. If Medea's guilt is to be identified with the lucid premeditation of the infanticide, which is the result of her conscious, autonomous action, in *Beloved* the *furor* that propels the gesture and the speed with which it is carried out, leaving no time for thought, make Sethe a character newly innocent in her tragic essence.

Medea, in fact, cannot justify her horrifying crime as imposed by fate, or committed for ethical values beyond her will: on the contrary, she is conscious and responsible, free and disobedient. She was not the first murderous mother in literary and mythological tradition: other tragic figures preceded her in performing this terrible act[43]. What makes her such a scandalously unique figure in tragedy is the firm resolution with which she declares: «I will kill my sons» (Medea: v. 792) and in the rigor with which she faces the unhappy destiny that she, and, for the first time, not a divinity, has decided on. Unlike Medea, Sethe's gesture is not coldly premeditated, but bursts out impulsively, and yet with extreme lucidity: her action is not the result of a careful and impeccable design planned down to the last detail, but the final instinctive attempt to save her children. Sethe kills, aware that she has no alternative, and stains herself with the only crime that can be pinned on her: a mother's unbounded love. That is why the reader feels indulgence and compassion for her; the desperation and dignity of this tragic figure, apart from her terrible past as a slave and the profound suffering that derives from it, ensure her our absolute respect and most sincere pity. Unlike Medea, Sethe acts with clear-eyed determination, without half measures or inner laceration. Morrison's heroine, like Seneca's, kills only out of excess of love and

---

[43] We need think only of Althaea, Procne, Clytemnestra and Ino.

cannot be blamed for this: «I took and put my babies where they'd be safe» (*Beloved*: 164), she says[44].

The theme of infanticide in *Beloved*, then, has both Euripidean and Senecan values, to the extent that, as well as the reasons leading to the infanticide that Euripides lists without justifying them, Morrison, like Seneca, adds elements that exculpate her. In this way, although Sethe is guilty of a cruel and profoundly unjust act, the reasons for it support and justify it so much as to arouse the reader's pity. Having no other choice, and with a Machiavellian determination to achieve her one aim at any price, Sethe kills out of love, and carries out her revenge on the strength of this love.

The solution of infanticide allows Sethe to prevent her daughter going through the horrors of slavery, and to oppose slavery in its basic premise: the negation of individual identity. Slavery taught property as being the only paradigm for relations between human beings, and denied slaves any desire other than that of the master; in this scenario, Sethe performs a gesture that may be extreme and painful, but that imposes itself as a supreme exercise of the will to the extent that it overturns the very essence of slavery and allows her to vindicate her freedom without impediments. Sethe claims her right of maternity over the children who are hers alone, and no longer the master's, and replaces the social death of chains with the physical death that alone can break them. Killing her little girl, Sethe not only wants to ensure her freedom, no matter of what kind or at what price, but also to keep her to herself in a terrible, endless embrace. Precisely because slavery can separate her from her daughter, Sethe kills her so as not to be separated from her: and in this way her maternal attachment to the nameless child becomes a tragedy of separation and fusion, love and possession, that is almost as horrifying as slavery. Captivity and maternity therefore become impalpably adjacent in the novel, almost as if the mother were feeding on her daughter as the master feeds on the slave. Once again, the mother is defined in her vampire-like fusion with her child, feeding on the one who, paradoxically, absorbs her and satiates her:

---

[44] «None of us, if we love, can stop ourselves from the wish to kill» writes Martha Nussbaum in *Serpents in the Soul: A reading of Seneca's Medea* (1997: 222).

> I am Beloved and she is mine. [...] Beloved You are my
> sister You are my daughter You are my face; You are me
> [...] You are my Beloved You are mine. (*Beloved*: 210-216)

The highly complicated tie between Sethe and Beloved is typically pre-Oedipal, while the novel reveals the deepest and most destructive drives in a maternity that slavery has made extreme, treating the terrifying figure of a terrible mother who, once again, generates and devours, creates and destroys.

6. Guilt and Revenge: Going beyond the Myth and Returning to the Archetype

Sethe's only real fault is her deceptive, fallacious attempt not to remember. Through an incessant, unproductive activity of *disremembering*, in fact, she had tried to repress what had denatured her maternity. But what has been repressed returns disturbingly, re-embodied in the novel, animated with new life: the ghost of Beloved takes flesh and comes back to life, demanding to be recognized and remembered. Only by going through the pain of the memory again can Sethe reconcile herself with her past and look with new eyes to the future, replacing the self-destruction of Euripides' heroine with a genuine palingenesis. After expiating her sin, she can be rehabilitated to life and re-accepted within the community. Purified by suffering and transformed by the memory of a past that, however painful, is now distant, she can be readmitted to the life of the Afro-American community that had ostracized her.

> The singing women recognized Sethe at once and surprised themselves by their absence of fear when they saw what stood next to her. The devil-child was clever, they thought. And Beautiful [...] Her smile was dazzling. (*Beloved*: 261)

The character's catharsis takes place and is fully embodied only at the end of the novel, when the women of Cincinnati, forming a procession whose composition and function recall the chorus of classical tragedy, reach number 124:

> For Sethe it was as though the Clearing had come to her
> with all its heat and simmering leaves, where the voices

of women searched for the right combination [...]. Building voice upon voice until they found it, and when they did it was a wave of sound wide enough to sound deep water and knock the pods off chestnuts trees. It broke over Sethe and she trembled like the baptized in its wash. (IVI)

The reference to baptism gives particular symbolic value to the whole episode: Sethe is reborn to a new life as the baptized are re-born in Christ, and, reconciled with her present, can move toward her redemption. Sethe's only possible revenge emerges in the cathartic process of remembering. Through the enforced memory of the repressed event, Morrison forces Sethe, and all of us, to remember the 15,000,000 slaves who died in the Middle Passage[45]. The novel, in fact, is dedicated to the «Sixty million and more» – an invitation to retrieve a part of History that too many have forgotten or not wanted to remember. The process of healing from this collective amnesia that affects everyone without distinction, black and white, is a painful but necessary process to give a face to all those nameless, unremembered dead.

The element of revenge actually becomes a triumphant reassertion of her rights against the white master who had subjugated her, reducing her to slavery. Sethe, the black woman, like the Greek and – still more – the Latin Medea, is a mother who depends on someone else. The main function of motherhood – that of breast-feeding – is a universal cultural paradigm that, in ancient societies, as in the Afro-American society described by Morrison, always works to someone else's advantage. Medea brought up her children, only to have to offer them to the hostility of an enemy land, the horrors of war, or the dangers of military life; while Sethe seeks to defend her milk from the violence with which it is taken from her, and to nourish her children, who are destined to a life of slavery and violence.

---

[45] The «Middle Passage» of the Atlantic was plied by slave ships from the early sixteenth century to the end of the nineteenth century. In the long, inhuman voyage from the Gulf of Guinea to the Caribbean, before at last reaching the American continent, the Africans, branded and stripped, were chained and massed in the holds, where many of them died. It has been calculated around 20% of those embarked did not reach their destination: many died of hardship or disease, and others let themselves die of melancholy; on arrival, the survivors were auctioned off as slaves.

> I'll tend her as no mother ever tended a child, a daughter.
> Nobody will ever get my milk no more except my own
> children. I never have to give it to nobody else – and the
> one time I did it was took from me – they held me down
> and took it. Milk that belonged to my baby. [...] There
> was no nursing milk to call my own. I know that it is to
> be without the milk that belongs to you; to have to fight
> and holler for it, and to have so little left. I'll tell Beloved
> about that: she'll understand. She my daughter. The one I
> managed to have milk for and to get it to her even after
> they stole it. (*Beloved*: 200)

The novel's protagonist here refers to one of the episodes from her past regarding the flight from «Sweet Home», which resembles the flight of Medea and Jason from Colchis: before she manages to escape, pregnant with Denver, Sethe is captured by Schoolteacher's nephews, two white men who forcibly extract the milk from her breasts. In this connection, it is worth briefly considering the symbolic value of Schoolteacher and his two nephews in the novel: the three start working at Sweet Home after the death of Mr. Garner, with responsibility for the slaves, and at once the master's strange lessons become a sort of symbolic representation of an education in racial contempt, founded on the natural inferiority of the slave-animal.

The symbolic value of the episode of the milk sees Sethe deprived of the possibility of motherhood and, so, of freely bringing up her children in a racist society that justifies and legitimizes slavery. However, the violence of being deprived of her milk is accompanied by the determination to ensure that it never happens again: Morrison replaces Medea's inner conflict with all the rancor that derives from the need to satisfy a desire that has been repressed for too long: Sethe's to be a mother, and Beloved's to have a name. Significantly, the reader is informed of the resentment and rage that animates the action of both characters from the beginning of the novel: «124 was spiteful. Full of a baby's venom» (*Beloved*: 3). Both characters are moved by a slowly emerging but uncontrollable desire, which has been too long repressed, to repudiate slavery. And so, if Sethe claims her need to be a mother and bring up her children for herself and no longer for her master, the child's ghost, which is incarnated in the body of a young woman and demands to be recognized by being given a name, only requires to be loved as a daughter so that she can live again in the memory of all those who have wanted to forget the horrors of slavery.

If, then, the sacrifice of children in Euripides' Athens and, still more, in Seneca's Rome, represents the separation of the couple and the destruction of the man for whom these children had been born and brought up – the annulment of the only beneficiary of a union that is now destroyed[46] – in *Beloved* it represents the attempt to break a tie that is still too strong and resistant – to liberate herself, through the bodies of her children, from the fetters of slavery. The children belong to the master, and only in relation to him does maternity have meaning: no Afro-American mother before Sethe, her own included, had had any rights over her children, who were almost always born out of violence. In fact, Sethe says «I was the one she didn't throw away» (*Beloved*: 201), referring to her mother, who had abandoned all her other children as they were the fruits of white ill-treatment, but had wanted to save only her, who had been born from a genuine, deep union with the one man she had really loved and had wanted to marry. But blacks were not allowed to marry: like motherhood, it was not regarded as one of the sub-human activities that these inferior beings could aspire to. But, for Sethe, these children belonged to her alone and had no reason for existing if they had to go back to being the property of her master. The decapitation of the child, in fact, paradoxically represents the mother's only way of possessing her forever: it is as if, to be able to go on containing her inside herself and being one with her forever, Sethe could only separate from her forever, avoiding the pain of separation and incorporating her in an indistinct, regressive fusion.

In *Beloved* the repercussions of the enforced interruption of this bond are seen, first of all, from the mother's point of view: revealing the deepest and most destructive drives of extreme maternity, she stands at the same time as a model of integrity and steadfastness. Like Polynices in *Hecuba*, Sethe shows all the heroism of which a slave is capable, and also that she is truly superior to those who can

---

[46] As Gianni Guastella (2000:151) writes: (trasl.) «As we know, in Rome the birth of children was the declared aim of matrimonial unions: and was also what gave them material substance, combining the parents' blood (*socius sanguis*) in a single body. The alliance of the families was embodied (so to speak) in the newborn: and the children were thus significant proof of the shared tie between the parents, although their main function was that of prolonging the paternal stock».

only claim to be superior. Nobility and beauty lie in the courage of a slave and the heart of a barbarian from the East, in the daring of a foreigner and the brazenness of a subaltern: essentially, in the voice of a woman who dismantles the mystifications of power and subverts their implausible values and supposed qualities. The Greek nobleman, like the white master, is the one who is really capable of barbaric acts and abominable wickedness; the epic purport of the dominant culture and, with it, the legitimacy of slavery, is thus diminished in the rejection of any idea of Fate as the ordering principle of human actions and of slavery, insisting on the role of individual will and human responsibility in deciding the story.

What Morrison seems to retrieve from Euripides' Medea, then, are the original features of the chthonic Great Mother, drawing on the most archaic stratum of the myth, that in which Medea was still a strong, fearless woman. She replaces the strictly classical elements of the myth with the pre-classical ones of the archetype, inverting the traditional symbols of the literary myth and going back to its origins, which have often been either repressed or forgotten. The ravenous, voracious *Devouring Mother* appears intermittently throughout the text, transposed into Beloved's uncontrollable hunger:

> To go back to the original hunger was impossible. Luckily for Denver, looking was food enough to last. But to be looked at in turn was beyond appetite; it was breaking through her own skin to a place where hunger hadn't been discovered. (*Beloved*: 118)

With the rage of one who cannot assert herself autonomously, because she is unable to distinguish herself from and survive outside the maternal bond, what Beloved wants, more and more obsessively, is the mother's body, which she metaphorically devours until there is no more of it. Greedy and insatiable, she expands over her, incorporating her, to the point of consuming her in a total fusion, related to the dark original union of mother and unborn child.

> The ambivalent dialectic between fusion and separation is illuminated by the dialectic between the archetype of maternity and the historical experience of slavery, between maternal orality and the function of writing, be-

tween images of liquid fusion (blood, milk, water) and metaphors of separation (decapitation, strangulation)[47].

The pre-Oedipal fusion between Beloved and Sethe, which is threatened only by the intervention of Denver, whose voice is interweaved with theirs, giving rise to a surreal dialogue, is evident in many monologues in which the two characters seem to be fused and confused in a single, indistinct voice. The archetypal sound of song, the confused murmuring of prayer, the containable flow of water: in *Beloved* everything is orality and sound, fluidity and music, even visually in the final pages; everything seems to confirm the archetypal link between mother and daughter that is installed in the pre-Oedipal phase and that is impossible to break.

> I am Beloved and she is mine. Seethe is the one that picked flowers, yellow flowers in the place before the crouching. Took them away from their green leaves. They are on the quilt now where we sleep. She was about to smile at me when the men without skin came and took us up into the sunlight with the dead and shoved them into the sea. Sethe went into the sea. She went there. They did not push her. She went there. She was getting ready to smile at me and when she saw the dead people pushed into the sea she went also and left me there with no face of hers. Sethe is the face I found and lost in the water under the bridge. When I went in, I saw her face coming to me and it was my face too. I wanted to join. I tried to join, but she went up into the pieces of light at the top of the water. I lost her again, but I found the house she whispered to me and there she was, smiling at last. It's good, but I cannot lose her again. [...] Three times I lost her. [...] Now I have found her in this house. She smiles at me and it is my own face smiling. I will not lose her again. She is mine.

---

[47] (Orig.): «L'ambivalente dialettica fra fusione e separazione è illuminata dalla dialettica fra l'archetipo della maternità e l'esperienza storica della schiavitù, fra l'oralità materna e la funzione della scrittura, fra le immagini fusionali liquide (sangue, latte, acqua) e le figure della separazione (decapitazione, strangolamento)» (Portelli, 2004: 322).

Tell me the truth. Didn't you come from the other
side?
Yes. I was on the other side.
You came back because of me?
Yes.
You rememory me?
Yes. I remember you.
You never forgot me?
Your face is mine.
Do you forgive me? Will you stay? You safe here
now
[…]
Will we smile at me?
Can't you see I'm smiling?
I love your face.   (*Beloved*: 214-215)

                    […]

We played by the creek.
I was there in the water.
In the quiet time, we played.
[…]
I needed her face to smile.
I could only hear breathing.
[…]
She hurt me.
I will protect you.
I want her face.
Don't love her too much.
I am loving her too much.
[…]
She left me.
Daddy is coming for us.
A hot thing.

Beloved.
You are my sister
You are my daughter
You are my face; you are me
I have found you again; you have come back to me
You are my Beloved

You are mine
You are mine
You are mine

I have your milk
I have your smile
I will take care of you

You are my face; I am you. Why did you leave me
who am you?
I will never leave you again
Don't ever leave me again
You went in the water
I drank your blood
I brought your milk
You forgot to smile
I loved you
You hurt me
You came back to me
You left me
I waited for you
You are mine
You are mine
You are mine   (*Beloved*: 215-217)

The Great Mother, beautiful and terrible because she incorpo-
rates and preserves everything in herself, is the expression of a female principle underlying matriarchy and therefore anterior to the
male principle on which Western civilization is founded. As patriarchal values developed, the female, and therefore negative, dimension
of the Female archetype was deliberately forgotten, and so primeval
figures like Circe or Medea were reduced and devalued to the point,
in some cases, of being completely repressed.

As an Afro-American woman, Morrison can only amplify the female dimension of myth and the mythological dimension in the lives
of women, particularly Afro-American women. In this way, the negative dimension of the Archetype, which has been written out of patriarchal civilization, is recovered in the light of primordial, female
elements: in this way, aspects of the myth that in the classical period,
and with Euripides in particular, were fixed in literature as the result

of androcentric, hegemonic conditionings, are replaced in *Beloved* with pre-verbal, pre-classical, *female* ones, of the myth itself.

7. New Trends and Female Re-readings: Celebration of Maternity

Theory has always abstained on Medea, and no psychoanalytical text, from Freud to Jung, has given her more than marginal attention. Medea has never been celebrated for giving voice to the repressed or to desire, nor has she been evoked to illustrate the Jungian theme of the ambivalence of the maternal. She therefore remains a tragic, disturbing figure whose terrible fascination is irresistible. Her cosmic, primeval power, her daunting, apocalyptic aura silences everything, while she escapes any single interpretation. In the second half of the last century, the link with the mother, which Freud did not give any particular attention to – though he recognized it as decisive for the child's development – was studied by many psychoanalysts, including Anna Freud and Melanie Klein. Vindicating the exclusively female characteristic of maternity, which for too long was determined by a patriarchal society, making it an oppressive institution, Adrienne Rich introduces the concept of matrophobia as the desire to escape the forces that had enslaved one's mother so as to become free, distinct individuals. In her celebrated, pioneering work *Of Woman Born: Motherhood as Experience and Institution* (1977) she writes:

> Matrophobia can be seen as a womanly splitting of the self, in the desire to become purged once and for all of our mother's bondage, to become individuated and free. Matrophobia [...] is the fear not of one's mother or of motherhood but of becoming one's mother.[...] But where a mother is hated to the point of matrophobia there may also be a deep underlying pull toward her, a dread that if one relaxes one's guard one will identify with her completely. (Rich, 1986: 235-6)

Matrophobia, then, does not mean fear of one's mother or of maternity, but fear of becoming *like* one's mother – like the woman who has transmitted and perpetuated all the restrictions and degradations of female existence. The relation between mothers and daughters, which, understandably, is rooted in patriarchal societies, remains an extremely open question, even when the pillars of those societies have crumbled and toppled, to the point of becoming an autonomous theme in contemporary women's writing. As Paola Splendore reminds us (2004: 185), only during the twentieth century did the relation between mothers and daughters and the representation of maternity become independent narrative themes, and not just mere corollaries reflecting stereotyped roles and patriarchal values.

Reassessing Freudian assumptions and re-reading the myth of Oedipus from a feminine perspective, female psychoanalysts and philosophers such as Julia Kristeva, Hélène Cixous and Luce Irigaray revalued in the 1970s the relation between mother and daughters, re-introducing it to an endemically male-chauvinist literary tradition. After rejecting parricide as the origin of culture (Freud, 1912-13) and, with it, the success of the Oedipus complex as almost entirely due to late-nineteenth-century Viennese patriarchal ideology (Brenkman, 1992: 929), Luce Irigaray defined matricide as being at the origin of patriarchy and, so, at the heart of Western culture. Preferring alternative myths to the over-interpreted and misinterpreted one of Oedipus, she thus re-read Aeschylus' *Oresteia* and drew from Agamemnon and Antigone sufficient evidence of the repression of the female and the maternal in favor of the patriarchal order. In S*peculum of the Other Woman* (1974) she deconstructed the structures of phallocentric culture and called on women to lay claim to their symbolic, verbal dimension.

If the female and maternity have been regarded as antithetical to modern intellectual and artistic activity, where the female artist had to deflect the femininity of her art toward dominant male values and regard her maternity as the only true form of creation, the Afro-American tradition stands apart from these assumptions and concentrates on the need of women to find their creativity in the unwritten creativity of their mothers. And so, rather than the most common aspects of maternity in representations of it in European literature (involving a conflict between mother and daughter), Toni Morrison prefers to celebrate it, as, for all the difficulties that the attempt to restrict it to narrative confines involves, it remains one of the basic themes of contemporary Afro-American narrative discourse.

In *In Search of Our Mothers' Gardens* (1983), Alice Walker exhorts black women writers to seek in the non-conventional forms of art of their mothers the spirituality, profundity of song and beauty of poetry with which they accompanied every kind of creation, every quilt made of scraps of material and colored patches[48]. Instead of the figures of mothers unable to mediate between their daughters and the outside world, because they lack any authority or social value, the Afro-American women writers offer images of strong women whose opposition to the oppression of slavery and whose repeated traumas of separation make them a real example to follow and connect with. Their power is born out of their trauma, and their narrative is built out of the chronicle of separation.

The maternal figure is therefore a metaphor of their origins, their belonging and their roots: returning to Sethe, Beloved is rejoining not only her mother, but her race and her history, the history of the «sixty million and more»[49], of all the slaves who died during the Middle Passage, to whom the novel is dedicated and who have never been honored by official memory. The ghost of the child, «the central figure of the intermediate space, straddling life and death, matter and immateriality, presence and absence, past and present»[50], returns *full of rancor*, to lay claim to the existence of a past that has been forgotten. Her rage echoes Sethe's, who, for as long as her condition as a slave persists, disinters her repressed desires and those of all the dead, forgotten slaves who wander like ghosts in an America intent on repressing a past that is too uncomfortable and unbearable.

---

[48] The *quilt* is a major theme in the novel, always connected with memory, emotions and the construction of identity.

[49] Actually, this is a literary exaggeration that is not borne out by the historical facts: we do not know exactly how many Africans were deported to the Americas between the late-sixteenth and the nineteenth centuries: the usual figures given are 15,000,000 slaves deported, and around 4,500,000 dead at the outbreak of the Civil War (1861-65).

[50] (Orig.): « [...] figura centrale dello spazio intermedio, a cavallo fra vita e morte, materia e immaterialità, presenza e assenza, passato e presente». (Portelli, 1996: 397).

8. Overcoming Myth and Slavery as the Resolution of a Conflict

And before I'd be a slave, I'll be buried in my grave, and go home to my Lord, and be free [51]

In the history of Western culture the conquest of identity and individual autonomy has often been recounted as the result of a conflict of generations between fathers and sons. The Freudian idea is that this conflict principally takes the form of a dramatic confrontation between authority and autonomy, and must ineluctably be resolved in the destruction of the relation between the protagonists, but this was questioned by later psychoanalytic studies in the second half of the last century, which tried to salvage its positive aspects. The conflict need not be modeled on stories of Western males and can be resolved outside the dynamics of war, and gaining identity and autonomy does not necessarily mean destroying a relationship, but may also be achieved through dialog.

There are, in fact, other ways of imagining the formation of identity and individual autonomy that do not involve a clash: we need to imagine what Iacono calls «autonomy in relation» (Iacono, 2004: 1), or, in other words, the «formation of an autonomy that does not need to eliminate the other or destroy the relation that ties the two of them, if it is to assert itself and, so, free itself from the bond of an authority that conditions and restrains it; on the contrary, it is achieved within that relation by transforming it» (IVI) [52]. Iacono notes how this idea, which Winnicott had developed and which was later taken further by the psychoanalyst Jessica Benjamin on the basis of the master-slave dialectic Hegel theorized in *Phenomenology of the Spirit* (1807), involves a shift in the role of the conflict between the poles of the relation in terms of change, not destruction.

---

[51] Refrain of *Oh Freedom*, a spiritual in which American blacks celebrated their freedom after the War of Secession in 1861. The author is unknown. It was recorded by Odetta («The Voice of the Civil Rights Movement») in 1956 and sung for the first time in public by Joan Baez for the March on Washington, August 28, 1963.

[52] (Orig.): « [...] formazione di un'autonomia che per affermarsi e, dunque, per liberarsi dal vincolo di un'autorità che la condiziona e la frena, non ha bisogno di eliminare l'altro, né di distruggere la relazione che lo lega a questo; al contrario, si realizza all'interno di essa, trasformandola».

> Hegel posits a self that has no intrinsic need for the oth-
> er, but uses the other only as a vehicle for self-certainty.
> This monadic, self-interested ego is essentially the one
> posited in classical psychoanalytical theory. For Hegel, as
> for classical psychoanalysis, the self begins in a state of
> 'omnipotence' (Everything is an extension of me and my
> power), which it wants to affirm in its encounter with the
> other, who, it now sees, is like itself. But it cannot do so,
> for to affirm itself it must acknowledge the other, and to
> acknowledge the other would be to deny the absolute-
> ness of the self. The need for recognition entails this
> fundamental paradox: at the very moment of realizing
> our independence, we are dependent on another to rec-
> ognize it. At the very moment we come to understand
> the meaning of 'I, myself', we are forced to see the limi-
> tations of that self. At the moment when we understand
> that separate minds can share the same state, we also re-
> alize that these minds can disagree. (Benjamin, 1988: 33)

In Hegel recognition of the other is an ironical effect of the master's omnipotence just when he is seeking self-confirmation in domi-
nating the other. Once the conflict has been overcome, usually with
the master's victory, the paradox of being recognized by the other,
and so depending on the other just as one is seeking to assert one's
own autonomy, is the *sine qua non* for individual autonomy being
created within the relationship and not by destroying it.

The Hegelian omnipotence of the master in Morrison's novel is fo-
cused in the bite, the brands, and the whip that marks the protagonists'
bodies and spirits, and once again sends us back to the cultural arrogance with which the West has always refused «autonomy in relation»,
strenuously opposing the displacement and expansion of the canon.
«Canon building is empire building. Canon defense is national defense.
Canon debate, whatever the terrain, nature, and range [...] is the clash
of cultures» (Morrison, 1989: 8). If canon building coincides with the
preservation of power, we can easily understand how the possibility of
existing inside the Western canon – white, autocratic and Eurocentric
– has been denied to any dissonant or dissenting voice that is not in
line with its precepts and models, and any kind of discussion or questioning of it has been essentially rejected.

What did happen frequently was an effort to talk about these matters with a vocabulary designed to disguise the subject. It did not always succeed, and in the work of many writers disguise was never intended. But the consequence was a master narrative that spoke for Africans and their descendants, or of them. [...] Whatever popularity the slave narratives had [...] the slave's own narrative, while freeing the narrator in many ways, did not destroy the master narrative. The master narrative could make any number of adjustments to keep itself intact. Silence from and about the subject was the order of the day. Some of the silences were broken, and some were maintained by authors who lived with and within the policing narrative. (Morrison, 1992: 50-51)

The tough master has put down any form of dissent with virulent passion (Morrison, 1989: 5) and with powerful weapons, but his conviction that he has settled things with his final victory is illusory as that conflict was actually inexistent:

The guns are very big; the trigger-fingers quick. But I am convinced the mechanism of the defenders of the flame is faulty. Not only may the hands of the gunslinging cowboy-scholars be blown off, not only may the target missed, but the subject of the conflagration (the sacred text) is sacrificed, disfigured in the battle. (IVI)

Jessica Benjamin brings out how, in terms both of power and learning, it is dangerous to leave the relation with the *other*, and at the same time how dangerous it is to fix the relation on an authoritarian basis.

[The] relation of destruction and survival is a reformulation and solution to Hegel's paradox: in the struggle for recognition each subject must stake his life, must struggle to negate the other – and woe if he succeeds. For if I completely negate the other, he does not exist; and if he does not survive, he is not there to recognize me. But to find this out, I must try to exert this control, try to negate his independence. (Benjamin, 1988: 38)

The process of gaining autonomy and perceiving oneself as other and the other as different from oneself takes place as part of the relation, that is to say, by changing and not severing the ties with the other. Recognition of the other might be a decisive step towards equal relations, starting from the affirmation of alterity.

> Now that Afro-American artistic presence has been «discovered» actually to exist, now that serious scholarship has moved from silencing the witnesses and erasing their meaningful places in and contribution to American culture, it is no longer acceptable merely to imagine us and for us. [...] We are not, in fact, «other». We are choices. And to read imaginative literature by and about us is to choose to examine centers of the self and to have the opportunity to compare these centers with the «raceless» one with which we are, all of us, most familiar. (Morrison, 1989: 8-9)

This, then, is Morrison's great challenge: to bear fitness to the extensive contribution that the silence of a people has brought to American culture and literature, reclaiming their dignity and asserting the urgency to tell their stories with their own voices. Drawing on what she is most familiar with, what she knows best, and what belongs to her, the myths that have already been told and the stories that have already been heard, Morrison brings to light what has been repressed and gives voice to what has been consigned to oblivion, relegated to the pre-symbolic dimension of the feminine and the maternal.

Yet even in this despair I have been pondering:
To kill myself would surely be a coward's act;
For he who cannot face the blows of Fate will quail
Before a spear held by a man. I will await
My death with patience.

(*Heracles*, vv. 1347-51, trans. Philip Vellacott, 1963)

Euripides' tragedy shows a gender conflict in the restless, contradictory setting of fifth-century Athens, which happens not only onstage, but in Medea's own psyche. Choosing a woman – and a barbarian woman at that – to dismantle archaic, self-destructive male heroism is a distinctive feature of Euripides' dramatic technique. Although he has often been wrongly accused of misogyny – both by his contemporaries and by modern critics – he was the first author in the ancient world to describe female figures in the intimate details of their human sensibility, and to present them in a positive light. He was the first to penetrate the most secret passages of female emotions, and to find, there, passions and fears there that are much more intense than their male counterparts.

Medea is a free and extremely modern woman, who defines herself not only by her autonomy and emancipation, but by exclusion and non-belonging: «I differ from many people in many ways» (*Medea*: v. 579), she had said to Jason in their first ferocious argument. In effect, her disposition is hard to shift, and her stubborn character does not admit compromises of any kind with anyone. She is remarkable for her ethical rigidity and her domineering individuality, but her diversity leads to ostracism. Sethe, too, a slave in her body but free in her soul, decides to act without qualms or remorse. Like Medea, she is a strong, determined woman, hot-tempered and passionate, decidedly unlike all the others. Just like Euripides' heroines, Sethe throbs with an irrepressible desire for freedom, and, no longer believing in Fate or any providential divine intervention, she takes her destiny into her own hands, wanting to have sole responsibility for her and her children's salvation. Not expecting either to be pardoned or pitied by her tormentors, she fights with the mere force of her solitude to assert the human dimension which she has been deprived of. In her long journey of pain and suffering, Sethe, like Medea, find the courage to free herself from the old habit of submission, whether physical or mental, and decides to resist indomitable to the end.

Like Euripides, Morrison appeals to individual responsibility, as glory and misfortune are not the result of divine machination or fatal predestination, but the consequences of man's voluntary action and free choice, exposed, as always, to the risk of error and failure. Sethe's journey as a woman in quest of self-fulfillment and self-affirmation, thus becomes the expression of the difficulty in achieving a broader, universal balance between men and women, white and black, masters and servants: a balance between past and present that extends to the whole of humanity and to every period of history.

Like Euripides, Morrison interprets the desolate laments of the excluded, the suffering of the offended and the solitude of the outcast: like Euripides, she chooses to tell the story through the voice of a woman, and a slave to boot, the lowest of the low, as the barbarian from Colchis was in Greece, to bear witness of the dignity of human beings and the irrepressible will to live. Although Sethe's infanticide may seem a surrender in the face of suffering, a kind of self-defeat of those who feel themselves defeated and simply give up living, it is actually the last, desperate attempt at resistance: and the return of Beloved, who obsessively demands a name and claims her right to life, confirms it.

That the protagonist is given no name is a clear sign of her confused identity and of the mixture of individual identities that conflagrate in a single, unbounded, fluctuating identity. The characters' identities intersect and blend with each other, often expressed in interchangeable dialog that gives rise to writing without confines and restrictions. In this way the narrative time involves different moments and phases, in which the narrating subject and the points of view constantly cross over, while the confused and extended identities are fused and confused, becoming a single one in the memory of a shared guilt and the refusal of an equal destiny. Everything in the novel is voice and writing: as the immaterial voice expands, it seeks a body and finds it in writing on the body; like the ghost, the voice and the sound seek substance and form, fixity and stability, in the body and the flesh.

Writing becomes both survival and resistance; it is linked with the body and struggles against invisibility and silence. That is why women narrate and, although they have been tortured, continue to narrate, like a mother who gives her life, wasting away, and whose martyrdom culminates in suckling (see Parat: 79-86). Through writing, Toni Morrison reclaims Sethe's hideously lacerated body, and it is her body that gives value to the writing, in a tireless fusion of solids and liquids, whites and blacks, voice and word. Once again, the phantasm of liquids saturates the novel by means of an infinite series of metaphors that contrast the flux of the voice and liquids with the fixity of writing, as if the author wanted to impregnate the text with sentiments and emotions, and then let it give birth to itself and the woman who generated it.

The persistence of the relation between language and writing, then, consecrates writing as legitimizing the female body in all its generative power: necessarily involving the maternal, the body-writing bond becomes a grand revelation of identity and mystery. The identity of the woman and the mystery of the life she tends are thus revealed in the creative act and in the birth of the text. As often happens in Liz Lochhead too, the irresistible, impetuous force of the act of living life is translated into the power of verse, and the act of procreation becomes the act of creation, birth becomes the birth of oneself in writing[53]. The monstrous, disturbing body of the woman is thus exorcized through writing, and, in it, exalts all its splendor and beauty.

> You only have to look at the Medusa straight on to see her. And she's not deadly. She's beautiful and she's laughing. (Cixous: 885)

---

[53] «She'll crumple all the tracts and the adverts, shred all the wedding dress-es, snap all the spike-heel icicles in the cave she will claw out of- a woman giving birth to herself» (Liz Lochhead, *Mirror's Song*, 1998).

CHAPTER THREE

Liz Lochhead's *Medea*:
Rewriting Language and Identity

> Is always two faced
> at best, she wished you
> into being. Yes, it was she
> cried at the seven drops of blood that fell,
> staining the snow-she
> who bargained crazily with Fate
> for that longwaited child
> as red as blood
> as white as snow
> and when you came true it was
> she who clapped her hands merrily because
> she was as happy as a Queen could be.
> But she's always dying early,
> so often it begins to look deliberate,
> abandoning you,
> leaving you to the terrible mercy
> of the Worst Mother, the one who married your father.
> She doesn't like you, she
> loves her sons.
> She's jealous of mirrors.
> She wants your heart in a casket.
> When she cuts the apple in two and selflessly
> takes the sour green half
> she's good and glad to see you poisoned
> by the sweet red pulp.
> Tell me
> what kind of prudent parent
> would send a little child on a foolish errand in the forest
> with a basket jammed with goodies
> and wolf-bait? Don't trust her an inch.

(Liz Lochhead, *The Mother*, 1979)

Classical drama in Scots translations continues to be used as a means to explore the range of new identities being shaped in contemporary Scotland. If the translations produced after the Act of Union in 1707 were rural in both themes and language, depicting Scotland only as a small and powerless part of a larger political unit, the translations that followed the establishment of the devolved Scottish Parliament and, as a consequence, the restitution of limited political powers to Scotland, aim at imagining Scotland as a new urban nation, though still homophobic, divided by tension and shattered by sexual repression. Through *Medea*, as through the major productions of translations of classical texts, the darker side of Scottish culture is indeed explored and questioned. *Medea* raises issues that require to be recognized and addressed in contemporary Scottish society through that of ancient Greece.

In order to delineate the cultural, literary and theoretical framework of Lochhead's writing, the present chapter, which mainly deals with her rewriting of Eduripide's *Medea*, will be limited to two basic conditions: her being female and Scottish. It will analyse how these two parameters of gender and nationhood determine her use of language, and how through language she revisits the template and retells the myth. The present work will thus be dedicated to what I consider the key concepts in Liz Lochhead's *Medea*, namely the definition of gender and identity through the use of Scots in the literary problem of adaptation. These aspects define and delimit the present work whose main aim is to allow Lochhead's work significant critical appraisal.

1. New Voices for Scotland: The Scottish Theatre «Renaissance»

The decade between 1963, when the first Traverse building was opened, and 1973, when the Scottish Society of Playwrights[54] was founded, includes such significant change within the Scottish theatrical tradition that it can certainly be defined as the Scottish «theatrical Renaissance». In this decade, the roots of contemporary Scottish playwriting are founded and, besides the earlier attention paid to a rather idealized rural and romantic view of Scotland, or to more striking contemporary issues, two main key strands in recent theatri-

---

[54] The Traverse theatre and the Royal Lyceum in Edinburgh were producing dramatic «experiments» mostly from Glaswegian playwrights, while the Scottish Society of Playwrights (SSP) is the national playwrights' support and development organization, representing theatre playwrights in Scotland.

cal scholarship can be identified: the conception of history and identity, and a new emphasis on writing in Scots.

By the 1970s, in fact, the Scottish theatre seemed to adopt two ways forward: the pursuit of the progressive urban approach, or the reclamation and de-romanticisation of the problems of Scottish history which is now being used as a means of examining current issues of oppression, identity and freedom. Whether earlier playwrights used the historical discourse to present a different version of Scotland's past, mostly of the times giving an epic, or even comic, version of it, post-1970 Scottish playwrights re-examine history and discuss its often idealized mythologies. They rewrite and question both values and myths embodied in the traditional version of Scottish history, and in so doing rethink and redefine Scottish identity.

In such a scenario, the influence of the Edinburgh Festival[55] which produced new Scottish historical drama within an international context, played an important role and represented a new path in literary productions which had been completely neglected in the textual forms. The historical drama, in fact, became the way through which the long ignored national culture was eventually asserted and distinguished from English or British cultures, and through which Scotland could proudly demonstrate that a separate history exists. The importance of growing from their own roots and the fact that Scotland might someday give its own contribution to the world drama by cherishing its own national peculiarities, language included, can thus be finally and strongly asserted.

In a similar new perspective, many translations and adaptations from classical masterpieces of world drama spread out into the repertoire of plays in Scots. And in so doing, the Scots language, which had so long been given less dignity and importance than English, started to assert its power and range, and to affirm itself as a proper target language. Thus, following the Renaissance tradition, Scottish speech remerged as an artistically viable language, and all its varieties and idioms potential began to be largely explored.

---

[55] The Edinburgh Festival Fringe was started in 1947 with the intention of helping international relations in the aftermath of the war, but it soon turned to be the most important event in the development of the Scottish theatre. Without official support, it brought to Scotland new contemporary world drama from many different countries and traditions, allowing dramatists and actors access to an international culture from which they had been largely excluded.

Moreover, since 1970, translations into Scots have been taking place to an unprecedented extent and the Scottish theatre has hence been undergoing a real revolution and a self-conscious re-invention. Another important change in the Scottish theatrical Renaissance which highlights the widening of interests of Scottish theatre writing is the emergence of women dramatists, who had been rare in professional theatre until the 1980s. Until then, in fact, the scene had been characterized and dominated by the male lyric voice, allowing no female participation[56].

The early 1980s productions and after see, in fact, a more and more considerable activity of women playwrights that witnesses the changes of Scotland's literary scene. Among the reasons advanced for the absence of women from poetry and drama until the 1980s has been their domestic lives and lack of higher education which relegated them to a private and marginal role in society, and did not allow them to participate into the high nature of poetry. Women could in fact not even aspire to the public voice of the poet until the 1970s, when some rare female voices started to merge. Needless to say that in such a neglected context, writing about women's experiences from the inside was no doubt unimaginable and out of question, as it would have meant writing about something fundamentally insignificant and, thus, not worth being written about. Furthermore, even when women started to write, they did not have a proper female tradition to follow, nor did they know which language to use among English or Scots. That is probably why, at the very beginning of their activity, they chose to use English and employ existing models to modify and adapt them for their own purposes.

It was not until 1972, when Liz Lochhead's *Memo for Spring* was first published, that a clear break with the male Scottish poetic tradition was made and a new female voice started to speak for Scotland. Liz Lochhead can be considered the first artist who started to «write woman», in as much as she offered a radical departure from the forms of previous Scottish poetry, and to focus on female experiences. Her commitment to questions concerning gender, tradition and language - which were main concerns of feminist discourse from the 1970s onwards - distinguishes her as the first Scottish female poet to

---

[56] Due to Calvinism's influence, Scotland literature had almost completely consisted of prose and poetry until the first half of 20th century, and male-authored drama works were as rare as the female ones.

speak in her own voice, and makes her a «flame carrier» for most Scottish women writer to come. Jackie Kay says about her:

> She was one of the first poets that I ever heard. I think that certain people are flame carriers for a whole lot of people to come after them. I would say that without Liz Lochhead I wouldn't exist. Lochhead was one of the first women poets that made it possible to speak in her own voice, which was a Scottish voice. (quoted in Gonzales, 2004: 107)

Liz Lochhead stands out as a real innovator for women's writing in Scotland, as through her, Scottish women writers find a new confidence in their gender and their craft. They feel now mature to produce their own poetry which is completely diverse from their male counterparts' in both theme and style, and eventually speak in their own voice. Female productions, in fact, which totally transformed Scottish literary traditions, often address the ways in which male political and sexual power oppress women and limit their freedom of thought and independence of action. All the themes they are generally concerned with, be they historical or personal, are now clearly not male dominated. Yet, even though at present there are many Scottish women dramatists[57], still only a few plays by them have been published and only few of them have been performed more than once. That is why, in such a restricted panorama where the dissemination of plays by women is so strictly limited and governed by male publishers and directors, being the only woman writer so often produced and staged, makes Liz Lochhead no doubt the most popular and significant female Scottish dramatist of the second half of the twentieth century[58].

---

[57] To name only some: Jackie Kay, Kathleen Jamie, Ena Lamont Stewart, Joan Ure, and Jessie Kesson.
[58] This is, however, in itself problematic in a country which is still male-dominated and where being a woman writer means to «thrive in an adverse climate» (Hendry, 1989: 291).

2. Drama and Scots

> *The stage is not merely the meeting-place of all the Arts,*
> *but is also the return of Art to life*

(Oscar Wilde, *The Truth of Masks*)

During the twentieth century Scottish playwrights can only refer to very few limited models to develop their new form of Scottish drama. For about five hundreds years, in fact, David Lindsay's *Ane Satyre of the Thrie Estaitis* (1554) had been the only reference point for the Scottish playwrights, among whom very few were remarkable or successful. This stagnation was partly due to the status of Scottish language in general: after the Middle English period, and especially from the second half of the sixteenth century onwards, English replaced Scots as the language of religion first and of culture then[59]. Considered as an uneducated and corrupted dialect of English, Scots became more and more relegated in its usage, and even though some famous writers like Robert Burns and Sir Walter Scott employed Scots to depict the Scottish life, giving it dignity and value, it still remained the language of local and satirical depictions[60].

The rebirth of Scots as a literary medium, which is usually attributed to Hugh McDiarmid (1892-1978), only occurred in the early twentieth century, when Scots firstly flourished as a lyric language and then ended up to be the new voice of the dramatic productions. After World War II, in fact, Scotland started to feel the necessity to fill in all the gaps left unresolved by many historical traumas, and at the same time by the lack of a continuous literary tradition.

The attempt to come to terms with its past full of both historical and literary painful moments, and thus to recover its fragmentary

---

[59] The Reformation of 1560 and the fact that the Bible was no longer to be translated into Scots, saw the beginning of the language marginalization. The Union of the Crowns in 1603 and the removal of the court further reduced Scots' status to the extent that, when the Parliaments were united in 1707, it had no longer a place in the official discourse and became a predominantly oral language.

[60] The *Gentle Shepherd* was the first opera performed in Edinburgh in 1729. It was written in Scots by Allan Ramsay (1686-1758) who, as an advocate of Scottish nationalism, revived the interest in vernacular literature and directly inspired the genius of his greater successors.

history and identity, brought Scotland to long for its lost origins and its neglected past. Such a strong national revival, which is the result of the long displacement of Scotland's culture by England, is represented and synthesised by two deeply intertwined and already mentioned phenomena: the so called «theatre Renaissance» and the use of Scots as a new literary means. The «renaissance» of the linguistic potential of the Scottish language, for several centuries dismissed and lost, occurs alongside with the «theatre renaissance» that the Scottish scene has been undergoing since the 1970s. Being drama, in fact, a speech-based genre, it was the best means to explore and demonstrate the vitality of the vernacular, and since language is the first expression of a nation's history and culture, the claim for Scots undoubtedly becomes the major claim for Scottish identity.

Furthermore, after the Second World War the mass media were deeply shaped by the centralisation required by government control of broadcasting, and thus rigidly organised within an English oriented society still closed and hierarchical; in most radio and television programs Scottish identity and culture were regarded as stereotypical and ridiculous. There was little space for serious engagement with Scottish experience, and this lead audiences to turn to live theatre as the only means able to speak their own language and to communicate the new representations of their Scottish identity. Subverting the long established conception according to which all dramatic performances in Scotland had to be suppressed due to their inherent evil nature[61], theatre became a driving force for Scottish cultural change.

Hence, the weakest of Scotland's literary tradition became paradoxically the most incisive and loved, with a new generation of dramatists emerging to develop the new accents of a liberated Scottish voice. The unprecedented growth in the writing and performance of indigenous drama can be thus seen as part of the same resurgent national confidence. Quoting Young's words:

> [A]fter prolonged coma, Scotland is waking up, and the Renaissance in Lallans is [...] one manifestation of this process. (Corbett-Findlay, eds., 2005: 14)

---

[61] Because of the restrictive censures of Calvinism, theatre in Scotland was a more private than public event, and it was not until the eighteenth century that permanent playhouses were established.

3. Translating into Scots

The sixteenth and twentieth centuries have been the two key periods in the history of literary translation in Scotland. According to John Corbett, in fact, they both have been «times when the process of national refashioning was at its most urgent» (1999: 7), and in such a context translations from other languages revealed to be particularly useful, as they «helped fashion and refashion the self-image of Scotland» (IVI), that is to shape its own culture in relation to the culture of others and effectively place contemporary Scottish writing in a simultaneously Scottish and international context. It has, of course, been commonly observed that both personal and social identities are often defined in comparative terms, and that national identity may commonly be defined in relation to an imagined other[62].

The second half of the twentieth century - whose body rivals in both quantity and quality the original work written in Scots, and thus states its important contribution to modern Scottish literature and drama - has though been the richest period for translations into Scots. According to Randall Stevenson (and Wallace, eds. 1995: 4), Scots has in fact become the most fundamental influence on drama in recent decades, and indeed, alongside the original plays in Scots, translations into Scots have played an important role in «placing the language at the heart of modern Scottish drama» (Corbett-Findlay, eds., 2005: 8), and consequently exploring the creative resources of Scots as a target language.

If we understand the act of translating not only as a mere transposition of meaning from the source language, but as a creative and artistic process through which the target language is enriched and reconsidered, this becomes particularly true for Scotland and the definition of the Scottish identity with all its cultural and political implications. Since each translation into Scots is a way to rethink what it means to be Scottish, and since Scotland's political structure has undergone continuing transformations in the last century, we can assert that the «translation of drama into Scots [should be considered] essentially a twentieth-century, post-war development» (Findlay, 2000: 35).

---

[62] Since Scottish identity has always been a question of difference rather than of identification, translations into Scots have become more and more frequent in the Scottish literary activity as fundamental in the construction of the new national consciousness.

In the twentieth century, in fact, writers seem to have turned to translation into Scots with more energy and enthusiasm than ever. «Translation has played a crucial role in the theatre since the 1950s[63] because it is the link between the linguistic diversity of Scottish experience and the capacity of the indigenous theatre of a small European nation to absorb and reflect the international stage» (Smith, 1998: 305).

Whether translations are central to the literary activity of emerging nations and developing countries or not - the function of translation, in fact, being to «reinforce genres and offer opportunities for stylistic extension» (Corbett, 1999: 183) – they are marginalized in countries already settled and established (the vernacular is in fact quite rare in the English-language theatre beyond Scotland). Dialect translations can be considered as exclusive solutions adopted by «minority cultures» to have people accept as natural the representation of foreign plays in such a range of non-standard medium.

Dialect texts would in fact prove performable and theatrically effective to Scottish spectators, and thus be considered authentic and authoritative for their target audience. As Graham McLaren said about *Thebans*, in continuing a project already started with *Medea* he wanted

> to convey what these plays have to say to audiences today, as immediately as possible – to rearticulate ancient Greek drama for a contemporary Scottish audience. [...] With *Thebans* we tried to build on the lessons we had learnt about Greek drama, and continue to experiment and learn so that we could create something that would move and touch an audience. (Lochhead, 2003, Intro)

As noted by Corbett (1999), translations and Scots Renaissance writers can be all considered as responses to fundamental political changes in Scotland. «Lallans[64] is a language of a nation. Hugh McDiarmid and others are restoring it in full vigour for all the pur-

---

[63] The period since 1945 has seen translations of works from the historic repertoire by authors such as Moliere, Racine, Ibsen, Kleist, Aeschylus, Euripides, Gogol, Brecht and many others.

[64] «Synthetic Scots or Lallans is a Scots which, although it is based on the everyday speech of the translator, might also incorporate archaisms, neologisms, borrowings, and calques to extend the range of vocabulary», (Corbett, 1999: 126)

poses of national self-expression» (Young, 1946: 14). Vernacular translations, indeed, have grown indispensable for advancing the status and range of Scots, which is now recognized as a literary medium distinct from English, and can be therefore regarded as the language of the nation[65].

4. The Scottish National Theatre

The idea that Scotland should have a vibrant and vigorous National Theatre in order to boost the country's reputation abroad and benefit the people of Scotland, was discussed for many years and eventually featured in the National Cultural Strategy published by the Scottish Executive early on in the life of the new Scottish Parliament[66]. Consequently, the Scottish Arts Council set up an Independent Working Group to report on the feasibility of various models. Their findings were published in May 2001 and a commissioning model was adopted by the Scottish Arts Council two months later[67].

As stated by the then Scottish Arts Council Chairman James Boyle, the intent was to «see a brilliant and dynamic Scottish National Theatre which [would] build on stronger foundations for drama in Scotland and win prestige within [the] country and beyond by producing new writing and world-class productions. [...] A first-rate Scottish National Theatre which [would] be a credit to Scotland and its people»[68].

On this regard, the then Culture Minister Frank McAveety declared that the «National Theatre of Scotland productions [would] be created from the best of [Scottish] theatrical and writing talent, and made widely accessible to audiences across Scotland. [The Scottish]

---

[65] Some Scottish writers, among whom Douglas Young and Robert Kemp, were committed to the standardization of Scots and the adoption of «The Scots Style Sheet», drawn up in 1947. (See also note n. 51 in Corbett and Findlay, eds., 2005: 32).

[66] Scottish Executive, Creating Our Future, Minding Our Past: Scotland's National Cultural Strategy, 2000 (http://www.scotland.gov.uk/Resource/Doc/158792/0043111.pdf, last access 5th March, 2013).

[67] See Scottish Arts Council (2001) *Scottish National Theatre: Report of the Independent Working Group* (http://www.scottisharts.org.uk/1/latestnews/1001911.aspx, last access 5th March, 2013).

[68] Scottish Arts Council (24 July 2001) *A National Theatre for Scotland to be proud of* (http://www.parliament.uk/documents/commons/lib/research/briefings snpc-03000.pdf, last access 6th march, 2013).

talent deserves and needs this bigger stage to work on. [The NTS would] provide a showcase for the best of Scottish theatre and will create work of international significance which will represent Scottish culture abroad»[69].

So it happened: every intent was fulfilled and the National Theatre was eventually born. Created by consensus within an existing theatre community as well as by the political will of the new born Parliament, the National Theatre of Scotland was set up in 2004 and launched in February 2006[70]. Since then, a wide range of Scottish artists and companies have been commissioned to produce excellent work, drawing on a strengthened infrastructure which includes independent artists, producers, promoters, as long as building-based theatres and touring theatre companies. Furthermore, the upsurge of creativity, which needless to say had depended on multiple factors, has been encouraged by various levels of state and regional funding: money has been assigned to theatre companies and playwrights, and the Scottish Arts Council has been promoting Scottish culture both at home and abroad[71]. As intended by the Scottish Arts Council's model, the Scottish National Theatre started to provide a platform for Scottish drama as a whole: since its very beginning, it has been delivering higher quality work, building audiences in Scotland and getting in this way international recognition.

Proposals to promote Scottish culture at home and internationally, as well as boost literature, publishing and promoting Scottish literature across Scotland's schools, were eventually approved by Culture Minister Fiona Hyslop on February 7th 2011 when, respond-

---

[69] Scotland's National Cultural Strategy Annual report 2003 http://www.scotland.gov.uk/Publications/2003/11/18580/29640, last access 6th March, 2013).

[70] It is quite original, and democratic at the same time, that the new National Theatre is conceived as a «virtual» body, with only a few number of permanent staff and no single-based building of its own. Since its launch in 2006, the NTS has been involved in creating more than sixty-seven productions in over one hundred different locations. In so doing, the five official companies take theatre all over Scotland and beyond.

[71] Writers in Scotland often benefit from the chance of being «writers in residence» in theatres or universities. Liz Lochhead used to be such at Edinburgh University first and at Glasgow later.

ing to the Literature Working Group[72], she endorsed Creative Scotland[73] with the lead role in implementing the recommendations and outlined steps being taken to support the sector. She said:

> Scotland's distinguished literary culture is a notable part of our national identity. We have produced more writers per head of population than any other artform. It is now time to ensure this rich legacy is maintained and strengthened in future years. We will work with Creative Scotland to ensure that happens[74].

Being a superb advocate for Scottish literature, Liz Lochhead has been appointed new «Makar» of Scotland: she will thus be commissioned to produce a work for the 2012 Commonwealth Day Observance, and she will work with Creative Scotland to promote Scottish literature throughout Scotland and abroad, ensuring the full potential of the role is realised.

---

[72] The Literature Working Group was set up in 2009 and it was tasked with recommending a new approach to public sector support for literature, focussing particularly on writing and publishing. The Group was asked to examine the provision, both financial and nonfinancial, for all areas of literature: fiction, poetry, non-fiction, journalism, children's books, and any other forms of writing that are published in book or journal/magazine form, whether in English, Scots or Gaelic. It was also asked to address the needs of publishers and literary magazines; and of festivals, libraries, and all bodies working to promote literature.

[73] Creative Scotland is the national organisation responsible for Scotland's arts, screen and creative industries which came into being on July 1st, 2010.

[74] For the full response see http://www.scotland.gov.uk/Resource/Doc/340871/0113157.pdf (last access 6th March, 2013).

5. The Play as a Political Act

> *Tragedy then, is an imitation of an action that is serious, complete,*
> *and of a certain magnitude [...] through pity and fear effecting*
> *the proper purgation of these emotions.*

(Aristotle, *Poetics*, 6, transl. Applebaum, 1997)

In 2000, one of Scotland's leading theatre companies (Theatre Babel, founded in 1994 and directed by Graham McLaren), along with three of its leading playwrights – David Greig, Tom McGrath and Liz Lochhead – won Lottery Funding[75] to produce modern versions of Greek tragedies for a contemporary Scottish audience. In having three major Scottish playwrights adapt ancient plays for the Scottish audience, Graham McLaren's main intent was to

> create lasting work that would impact on Scottish cul-
> ture. [He] wanted to commission writers that could truly
> articulate the principal elements of the myths, and so
> create plays that would transform great and ancient clas-
> sical works into pieces that would speak not only directly
> to a Scottish audience but also of universal modern expe-
> rience. (Lochhead, 2000b, Intro)

With the «Greek project», he thus wanted to create plays that would directly speak to the Scottish audience and impact on the Scottish culture, contributing at the same time to creating a new drama tradition for Scotland as well as boosting a national political awareness.

In Scotland, there is no great tradition at all of the Classics. For the last three or four hundred years, you travel from Edinburgh or Glasgow, go a few hundred miles south, and every bugger seems to be doing Hamlet in their back room or in some courtyard or some-thing. Up in Scotland, nothing. So I had this idea that we could do a Greek project. As you may know, there are some political changes in Scotland at the moment, and one of the questions that occurred to

---

[75] See Scottish Arts Council Project and Lottery Grants (September 2001), (Edinburgh, September 2001) *Project and Lottery Grants* (http://www.scot tisharts.org.uk/resources/publications/past_awards/pdf/AwardedGrantsSe p01.pdf, last access 5th March, 2013).

me is - «how important are these plays in forming public opinion?» - so it was a kind of political act. I'd commissioned a version of «Oedipus», and I'd got David Grieg to have a look at that; «Electra», Tom McGrath; and «Medea», Liz Lochhead, (and for those of you who don't know, we've been hauling «Medea» around the country ever since). [...] I've been here, unusually, for the last two days and one of the things I'm quite keen on is that we all, in the questions and answers, try to speak the same language[76].

Graham McLaren openly asserts that he was influenced by political considerations and hence seems to be motivated by a kind of cultural nationalism. Those years were in fact the post-devolution ones, and Scotland was going through important political and cultural changes. The political process of devolving the nation and, as a consequence, of United Kingdom constitutional change, raised concerns about the potential or impending crises of national identity. Concerns that devolution and the establishment of a Scottish Parliament would lead to a decline in British identity and to a rise in Scottish identity, were expressed, and increased calls for Scottish political independence feared. Nonetheless, after many «unsuccessful attempts to introduce Devolution in Scotland and Wales in the 1970s[77], many Scottish pro-devolution bodies joined together to form the Scottish Constitutional Convention. [...] Its first meeting was held on 30 March 1989 and it adopted a declaration to assert the right of the Scottish People to secure an Assembly or Parliament for Scotland. [...] The Scottish Referendum on devolution took place on 11 September 1997 and the turnout was 60.4% of the electorate, with 74.3% voting for a Scottish Parliament» (Parliament and Constitution Centre, 2004).

After many fears and struggles, the Scottish Parliament was eventually born but the political and cultural identity it wanted to represent still remains inevitably elusive and indefinable. Over the centuries, many Scottish writers - from the medieval William Dunbar through Robert Burns, Walter Scott and R.L. Stevenson, to the twen-

---

[76] «Didaskalia, Ancient Theatre Today», «Panel Discussion on Complex Electra», Peterhouse College, Cambridge, 13-14 October 2001), 5.3, (Summer 2002), http://www.didaskalia.net/issues/vol5no3/trans02.html last access 5th March 2013).

[77] In a 1979 referendum, the Scots voted in favour of the Labour government proposals to establish a Scottish Parliament. Devolution was though rejected, as only 32.9 per cent of the electorate had voted in favour of it.

tieth century Edwin Muir and Hugh MacDiarmid - have drawn on their experiences of Europe and the rest of the world in order to question and define their sense of nationhood, trying in return to express to the world what it also meant to be Scottish. In so doing, they retained a sense of identity which has always been defined through diversity, lack and difference. National identity cannot be univocally defined and thus, using the words that La Corbie pronounces at the very beginning of *Mary Queen of Scots Got Her Head Chopped Off*, it can be offered a wide set of possible definitions:

> *Country:* Scotland. Whit like is it?
>
> It's a peatbog, it's a daurk forest,
>
> It's a cauldron o' lye, a saltpan or a coal mine.
>
> If you're gey lucky it's a bricht bere meadow or a park o' kye.
>
> Or mibbe… it's a field o' stanes.
>
> It's a tenement or a merchant's ha'.
>
> It's a hure hoose or a humble cot. Princes Street or Paddy's Merkit.
>
> It's a fistfu' o' fish or a pickle o' oatmeal.
>
> It's a queen's banquet o' roast meats and junkets.
>
> It depends. It depends… Ah dinna ken whit like *your* Scotland is.
>
> (Lochhead, 1999: 11)

In recent years and in contemporary drama a great number of dramaturgical questions related to politics, representation and above all identity arise along with the development of infrastructural investment and changes initiated by the new devolved Parliament. Devolution has in fact led to many direct shifts within Scotland's cultural infrastructure – which has been the subject of much governmental attention and interest - among which the launch of the National Theatre should no doubt be considered as the most groundbreaking and significant.

> Scotland has voted to redefine itself as a nation. To redefine ourselves we need to understand ourselves, exchange ideas and aspirations, confront enduring myths, expose injustices and explore our past. The quality, accessibility and immediacy of Scottish theatre make it one of the best arenas in which these dialogues can take place. (Harrower-Greig, 1997: 15)

The intention to enhance national and cultural identity through confronting the past and with rest of the world made the NTS the best place where to fulfil such premises and look for growth and improvement. Even though neither Tom McGrath's nor David Grieg's versions of Sophocles' templates are written in Scots, they both brilliantly fulfil Graham McLaren's intention to be versions of Greek tragedies for Scottish audiences of today. On this concern David Greig writes:

> When Theatre Babel approached me in 1998 with the idea of adapting Sophocles' *Oedipus The King*, I was very clear that I didn't want to do a translation. Apart from the fact that there are many fine translations in existence already, I didn't feel artistically inspired by the idea of literary authenticity. I was far more interested in emotional authenticity. I wanted to find a world in which I could re-tell Sophocles' story so that it would feel to a modern audience just as shocking, violent and nihilistic as if it were one of the so called «In Yer Face» plays which were dominating the British theatre at that time. I didn't want the audience to watch with their fingers stroking their chins, pondering the fineness of the poetry. I wanted them to reel back on their seats. I wanted to re-capture the first feeling I had on reading Oedipus as a child: the pity and terror, the catharsis. (Greig, 2005, Intro)

Graham McLaren had «three playwrights adapt classical texts in the light of the flourishing of theatre arts in the years before and following devolution and the re-convening of the Scottish Parliament after a gap of almost 300 years» (Hardwick, 2003: 80), in order to boost national identity through theatre and rewriting of ancient drama. Even though it has been suggested that the achievement of political goals limited and narrowed the cultural demand, the period between 1979 and 1997 was extremely fertile for Scotland, its writers and its productions.

After the Referendum, in fact, many books dealing not only with Scottish affairs, but with a wider cultural agenda, have been published. In such a scenario, Liz Lochhead's rewriting of *Medea* into Scots should be intended as both a means to enhance Scottish national identity, and as a further contribution to broadening the reborn Scottish literary tradition. Indeed, it helps to keep the language alive, demonstrating its creative potency and potentialities, and enabling Scottish audiences to confront and appreciate the resources of their own language. At the same time, it paves the way to the advancement of a distinctive Scottish drama: it contributes both the repertoire of Scots translations and it also contributes – as adaptations in general do- to the production of dramatic texts and to the collection of indigenous drama.

Without the political act the play would be demeaned. Liz Lochhead's *Medea* is not, in fact, just a play about a woman being scorned by her husband: it is not only about jealousy, rage and revenge. It is more: it is a play concerned with being without a city and without a home, and about multiple identities coexisting in a single territory. It is a post-devolutionary attempt to re-examine Scotland's identities and its multicultural composition.

6. Identity and «Scottishness»: Retelling Old Myths from a New Perspective

> I still have more of that Scottishness to explore, perhaps because until recently I've felt that my country was woman. I feel that my country is Scotland as well. […] I want to stay here and renegotiate it. This place of darkness I acknowledge as mine; this small dark country. I can't whinge about it if I don't talk back to it, if I don't have a go. (Nicholson, 1992: 223)

Scottish identity has always been a matter of difference rather than of self-determination, and the development of a sense of «Scottishness» has always been interrupted by periods of identification with English culture, due to Scotland's profound political and cultural divisions between the Highlands and Lowlands which often orientated the southern territories towards the dominant English culture[78]. To be a split country between England and Scotland is perceived as one of the major Scottish issues by Liz Lochhead whose works show a high degree of sensitivity to the double marginalization of women writers in Scotland:

> In many ways I think that the big theme in Scottish liter-
> ature is the split, from *Justified Sinner* to *Jekyll and Hyde*,
> and I think that's natural if you're Scottish where you are
> half English, really. There's a bit of you who's internal-
> ized all of that, so you're English, but you're Scots. So
> two different halves of you talk to each other which is
> very similar to the states of the male and the feminine.
> The Scots is in some ways the position of being the fem-
> inine with regard to Britain. You know the Celt, the oth-
> er. Once again, we split again – in Scotland, the Celt is
> the feminine, the Scots is the male, the standard. I don't
> know where that leaves Scottish Celts. They're split, and
> split and split. (Todd, 1995: 90)

The condition of being a woman, and a woman writer, which is deeply felt through its connection to Scotland and its divided destiny, is in fact described as a phenomenon upon which hegemonic fea-tures are linked to patriarchal and gender attributes, with no place for the subordinated and marginalized group of women. As a conse-quence of such hegemonic subordination, female Scottish writers have experienced a double exclusion - from the English and from the male-dominated Scottish discourse - that is both cultural and gender marginalization.

> Scotland. Scottish women have their own particular
> complications with writing and definition, complications
> which derive from the general problems of being a colo-
> nised nation. Then, that wee touch extra. Their sex.
> There is coping with that guilt of taking time off the

---

[78] As John Corbett has noted, «Lowland Scotland defines itself in opposi-tion to the Highlands, while urban Scotland defines itself in opposition to rural Scotland, and Catholic Scotland defines itself in opposition to Protestant Scotland [...] Scotland as a whole defines itself in opposition to England» (Corbett, 2007: 337).

concerns of national politics to get concerned with the sexual sort: that creeping fear it's somehow self-indulgent to be more concerned for one's womanness instead of one's Scottishness, one's working class heritage of whatever. Guilt here comes strong from the notion we're not backing up our menfolk and their «real» concerns. Female concerns, like meat or mother's plate, are extras after the man and the weans have been served. [...] Nurture or be deviant and sorry. Pursue your own goals only if you acknowledge it as selfishness. [...] So, on top of working out how to write (which is hard enough), on top of the need to reinvent the wheel, on top of finding time, there's the guilt, the guilt. Always the guilt. (Galloway, eds. 1991: 5-6)

In order to free women from such a constricted and impotent role, and thus retell familiar stories from a different perspective, namely turning her female characters from objects to subjects, Liz Lochhead uses historical and literary-historical material to expose how history has long served the patriarchal order and its power. For this purpose, the project of rewriting Scottish history in a feminist way furthermore means to Liz Lochhead to break with the conventional notion of Scottish tradition as a source of positive values and tradition.

She distances herself from the majority of earlier revisions written by male authors which were only attempts to glorify and celebrate the past, and manages to present Scottish tradition as full of clichés and inventions which need to be modified from within. In *Mythologies* Roland Barthes had already suggested that the best way to tackle myths is by elaborating them in a new, creative way and thus by inventing other stories out of the existing material. In so doing, the nature and the ideological intentions of the original myth are questioned, while a new, stronger one is created[79]. In a similar perspec-

---

[79] «Truth to tell, the best weapon against myth is perhaps to mythify it in its turn, and to produce an artificial myth: and this reconstructed myth will in fact be a mythology. Since myth robs language of something, why not rob myth? All that is needed is to use it as the departure point for a third semiological chain, to take its signification as the first term of a second myth. Literature offers some great examples of such artificial mythologies. [...] It

tive, if we consider myth as system of power, in as much as it can impress on people's mind and determine their thoughts and behaviour, Judith Butler's theory according to which systems of power can only be subverted from within (Butler, 1990a: 270-282) might be a further help in understanding both the link between repetition and subversion in feminist writing, and the reasons why so many women writers have turned their attention to the genre of adaptation.

Moreover, considering that repetition always involves a potential for difference (Deleuze, repbl. 2001), retelling old stories can often determine cultural change. Manipulating the myth, in fact, which is generally an alternative storytelling, can be potentially subversive and adversarial. When Liz Lochhead turns back to the past in order to «resignify» and renegotiate the present, she is in line with both the feminist writing and the new tradition of historical drama in Scottish literature, which is the most direct way to retell the past in a new, original manner. Historical drama is retold and rearranged as old myths and legends. Adapting a pre-existing text, be it fictional or historical, no matter whether it is a literary inter-text to be adapted or the factual past to be retold, represents the attempt to transform a pre-existing material and freely reinterpret it according to new formulas.

> I felt free to deviate from the original if I wanted. It was going to be a version of Medea, not a translation of Medea. I didn't feel I needed to stick to anything I didn't want. [...] I took the Euripides' myth and made a version for a Scottish company to do. (Pugliese, unpbl.)

Liz Lochhead's drama, whose core part is concerned with pre-texts adaptation, is therefore an attempt to rewrite stories in order to shape new identities and give voice to silenced people. Having accepted the invitation to rewrite Medea, she thus tries to mould the text to best address the issues presented and voice her concerns about women and the nation. Through her extraordinary capacity of appropriating the myth of Medea and making a new version of it, Liz Lochhead shows that the best way to fight the restrictive myths that define women and limit their culture is by tackling them on their own ground.

---

is what could be called an experimental myth, a second-order myth» (Barthes, 1972: 135).

In so doing, she impacts on Scottish culture and gives her own contribution to the cultural change which Scottish society is under-going, offering a possible alternative for Scottish women towards freedom and independence. The link between past and present is certainly not accidental and the nexus between reinterpretation and the power of reinterpreting is deeply connected to the problem of identity and self-consciousness.

7. Liz Lochhead and Scotland: Speaking the Nation in her Own Voice

In such a scenario, Liz Lochhead defines herself as one of the major Scottish female voices. Among the new Scottish female voices she is undoubtedly the most representative and the most represented, and thus, she has to be regarded as one of the leading figures in both Scottish poetry and drama. She is fundamentally a poet of language: she is fascinated by the way in which clichés, stock phrases and lin-guistic habits determine people's conception of the world, the way they perceive it and the opinions they build upon it. Much of her production is indeed concerned with the way people try to fit lan-guage to their ends and how they use it to shape the world around them. She employs everyday language in order to discuss and cun-ningly subvert it: her range of language, which is clearly female and Scottish[80], is used to satirise the difference between men and women, England and Scotland, and it is connected with gender, class and nationhood.

Her work, in fact, has to be placed and understood within the specific and cultural context of Scotland - since she quite often refers to Scottish history and employs Scottish language - and as the result of the female voice, most representative of both the theatre Renais-sance and the emergent woman literature. Liz Lochhead defines herself as a female author in the predominantly male dominated Scottish literary scene, highlighting the difference from the existing male tradition and attempting to speak the unspoken rules of posi-tions and identities.

She tries to create other, more desirable images of women, rather than accept the old clichés in which male writers have often depicted and stigmatized them. She excavates lost female voices from the

---

[80] «My language is female-coloured as well as Scottish-coloured» (in Somer-ville-Arjat, - Wilson, eds. 1990: 11).

dominant discourse and tries to give voice to the silences and gaps which history has never told. For this purpose, she uses past stories and history only as a starting point for her drama adaptations and rewritings: she exploits the genre of the historical play and the method of adaptation and revision to fight out the battle between tradition and invention[81]; and she often employs Scots to explore problems of linguistic, social and cultural marginalization of Scottish culture and language.

While rewriting Moliere, Chekhov, and Stocker she demonstrates her continuing interest in translation and above all the remarkable power of Scots as a target language. She thus rewrites the plays and at the same time re-invents the language. As she writes in her own introduction to *Tartuffe*, her Scots is «a totally invented, theatrical Scots, full of anachronisms, demotic speech from various eras and areas» (Lochhead, 1986). Scots is used to raise questions about gender, history, culture and language: in a word, national identity. Her translations subvert the *status quo* by redefining the multiple voices, speech communities and subcultures by which the nation is represented.

It is, in fact, significant that her poem collections, from the very first one *Memo for Spring* (1972) to the later ones *Islands* (1978) and *Bagpipe Muzak* (1991), are entirely written in English: whenever she is writing poems, and particularly the autobiographical ones, she indeed employs a variety of English which might no doubt be defined as standard. The lyrical inspiration seems thus to be strictly linked to the use of standard English rather than to Scots which, on the other hand, is more compatible with the notions of gender and nationhood. After all, English is the language in which she has been educated and which she probably feels is the language of authoritative poetry and of intimate, lyrical confession.

The reconfigurations of Scottish myths and legends provided by women dramatists and by Liz Lochhead are never used to evoke a lost Highland «never-land», on the contrary, the mythological world is used to interweave into the contemporary world and to redefine culturally constructed prejudices and stereotypes. Scottish women dramatists develop, in fact, their critical awareness of being women

---

[81] See Genette (1982), where the author makes a clear distinction between imitation and transformation of the mythological material. See also Judith Butler's concepts of repetition and resignification (1993).

and Scots and, above all, as Liz Lochhead does, they try to forge their female, Scottish and contemporary identities as writers.

Her dedication to Scotland and her prodigious dramatic activity which, as already stated above, has been strictly linked to the investigation of Scottish identity and culture through the use of Scots, in recent years has stolen time from her more private exercise of poetry. Her increasing interest in political issues and her intellectual commitment to left-wing politics are, in fact, strictly connected to the use of theatre as a more direct and lucrative form of literature and, as a consequence, to more democratic and popular forms of theatre, like pantomime and music hall[82].

In retelling what had already been told by men, Liz Lochhead evolves her new female mythology and starts to be a Scottish feminist writer, making the female equivalent to the nation[83]. As noted by Cairns Craig (1996: 355), «by the identification of her own condition with the country's, she makes redemption of the feminine equivalent to redemption of the nation». After all, Scotland has often been symbolized as female and now Liz Lochhead includes the female within the nation's narrative, employing Scots as its main language and thus having Scotland speak in her own voice.

8. Liz Lochhead's Revisionary Stance:
From Negation to Resignification

Whenever a poet employs a figure or story previously accepted and defined by culture, the poet is using myth, and the potential is always present that the use will be revisionist: that is, the figure or tale will be appropriated for altered ends, the old vessel filled with new wine, initially satisfying the thirst of the individual poet but ultimately making cultural change possible (Ostriker, 1986: 212-213).

All of Liz Lochhead's production is concerned with interpreting myth in a broad sense. Her revisionist stance and her demythologis-

---

[82] As David Hutchison has pointed out, during the twentieth-century performance forms as music hall and variety have been more successful in Scotland than anywhere else, probably because of their «fundamental dependence on a shared identity of experience between performer and audience». (1987: 164).

[83] «Being a feminist writer was stopping writing as if I might be a man, so being a Scottish writer is stopping writing as if I might be English» (in Somerville-Arjat.- Wilson, eds. 1990: 10-11).

ing approach to reality, which challenges the male assumptions from a feminist point of view, initiate the prolific reworking of classical masterpieces which, starting from *Blood and Ice* (1982) will proceed with *Tartuffe* (1986), *Dracula* (1989), *The Magic Island* (1992), *Three Sisters* (2000), *Medea* (2000), *Misery Guts* (2002) and *Thebans* (2003).

Dealing with archetypal literary types and figures taken from history and classical myths, or traditional folklore, fairy tales and biblical characters, she continually revisits old figures and myths, giving them new forms and meanings. She investigates the reasons behind the myth and the mythological discourse, trying to explore the modalities through which they still perpetuate themselves in the present with enormous success. In both her drama and poetry, in fact, she re-reads myths from a female and Scottish point of view, and uses them to analyse how sexual, social and national identities are constructed.

Myth is not only examined in terms of its meaning and content, though: it is also questioned as a form of employing language, namely as a form of expression, and as a way to tackle the past in order to change the present. Past and present are in fact two overlapping dimensions in her work and the way she addresses old facts, myths and archetypes is mainly a means to explore, question and subvert contemporary myths[84]. Through the use of shared myths which constitute our common background and define our culture, Liz Lochhead wants her dialogue with the present to gain a broader meaning and her voice a wider resonance. And since the myth extends personal experience to a more collective level, being a form of collective narrative[85], the rewriting of the myth becomes to her a way to obtain some sort of contemporary change.

Her revisionist mythmaking can therefore be considered a milestone in her whole production which, from its very beginning, appears to be concerned with the urge to «retell familiar stories from another angle» (Somerville-Arjat – Wilson, eds. 1990: 9). The pur-

---

[84] Barthes (1972) defines the contemporary myth as the complex of assumptions, stereotypes and *clichès* passively accepted by our culture which is thus uncritically defined and delimited by them.

[85] According to Plato's analysis of mythology in the *Republic, Laws and Dialogues,* myth is entwined in a texture of unofficial and oral culture in which it manifests itself as φήμη (voice). The mere and constant repetition of these «narratives» (often apocryphal and unauthorized) carried out by elderly people as grannies and nurses, at bed time or in the secret of dark places, transforms such «voices» in real myths and gives them the power to affect people's lives.

pose of «re-visioning» is thus to question the received opinions contained in the original text and to initiate a reinterpretation of the role of women as constructed and marginalized both by history and by the literary canon. In so doing, she reconfigures the historical and mythological events by forging new myths and new identities.

In *The Grimm Sisters* (1981), indeed, she has attempted to rewrite the very first version of reality men and women received from the realm of fiction (and to do this she has gone back to the stories children are told at bed time, those of the Brothers Grimm in particular), in order to show how much of them is generally taken for granted and how many received roles are the result of patriarchal and male-dominated conceptions about women and their ancillary role. In trying to give a contemporary turn to the traditional tales, Liz Lochhead employs colloquial register and slang expressions, which ridicule the pretensions of the original and, mocking the chauvinist attitude towards women, reflect the frustrated Scottish housewife's condition[86].

Almost all of her plays relate to the past and bring it back to life in a new, ironic way. Her plays refer to the historical past, they quote from it and play with the notion of tradition as such: in fact, in rewriting previous literary texts, she does not repeat cultural repertoires, but totally and ironically subverts them. In so doing, she uses tradition to transform it, giving in this way all her plays the tension between tradition and innovation.

As pointed out by Anne Kathrin Braun (2004: 59-84), in rewriting texts and old stories Liz Lochhead's revisionist attitude operates on different levels, which move from mere negation to mature creative «resignification». In *The Alternative History of the World, Part I* (*Bagpipe Muzak*, 1991), for instance, she simply retells and comments on the story of Adam and Eve from *The Book of Genesis*, offering a revision of historical and cultural clichés in rejecting prejudices and commonplaces. She does not offer any new suggestion, though, and her only aim seems to be the disruption and the *negation* of the source text, without creating any real alternative to it.

Another form of rewriting is the *alteration* of the original text. It implies less craft in adaptation and more wit in invention. Through text alterations offered in *The Grimm Sisters*, for example, Liz Lochhead renegotiates meanings and values, she refigures characters, and

---

[86] See above all *Mother, Spinster* and *Bawd*, in *Dreaming Frankenstein and Collected Poems* (1984).

shapes cultural clichés. Nevertheless, she is never definitive nor final, and she only suggests potential or possible alternatives. Her work is indeed full of irony and she is never entirely serious, as she perfectly knows that new interpretations can only upset texts, without ever replacing them. She thus uses the source texts as sources for figures and *personae* which still leave gaps and holes in the new story as well.

The third and actually the most important form of rewriting is the *resignification* of the template, a process in which both the author and the reader-audience take an active role. Its instances seem in fact the most radical in view of their attempt to subvert the predominant role system, as it serves to explain the subversion of cultural roles and of gendered inter-texts, and the creation of new, different identities. The process of texts' resignification implies the rejection of roles imposed by the gender or by the predominant culture and, at the same time, the attempt to «create the opportunity for a turn towards self-determination» (Braun, 2004: 83).

Nevertheless, the subversive effect might not be guaranteed and it might also result in a backlash, reinforcing the dominant system. The deconstruction of existing stereotypes and the presentation of alternative female images might in fact be problematic whether this brings parody, irony and criticism towards these new characters and contributes to create clichés and commonplaces around them. In rewriting old texts and redefining previous women roles, in fact, Liz Lochhead aims at having the contemporary, working-class, Scottish woman be self-defined, but at the same time, by this means she takes the chance to forge new and no less treacherous mythologies[87].

9. Revising Scotland's Cultural Myths

The question of revising cultural myths, which is surely a feminist concern, seems to be strictly linked to the notion of identity, and Liz Lochhead appropriates and negotiates Scottish literary tradition to tackle Scottish identity and nationhood. Her whole production is concerned with the deconstruction of the image of «woman» as presented by male-oriented and male-authored myths. Problematic motherhood and monster creation are investigated in *Blood and Ice*,

---

[87] Scotland's self-image is no doubt different from how it is perceived by non-Scottish people. It cannot be precisely the same as the stereotypical external image, even though it could also be the «homemade» result of Scotland's nostalgic vein which creates new, internal stereotypes.

while the extreme of monster-woman is presented in *Dracula*. In the former she demystifies the restraining myth of the idealized female figure, while in the latter she connects the menacing otherness of the vampire to the otherness of the female in a male-dominated culture. In both works, therefore, she exposes some myths of femininity as products of male imagination, and investigates through them the cultural construction of female identity.

The repressive agency of myth on women and the position of women who have always had to identify with male-authored models of femininity, takes on more contemporary connotations in *Mary Queen of Scots Got Her Head Chopped Off* (1989), where Scotland's position is compared to the woman's, in as much as they share the same destiny of repression and otherness. Being «other» to England, though, and being forced to identify itself under a model of false «Scottishness» created and imposed on it by the dominant English culture, Scotland has been reduced to the feminine and ended up being «other» to itself. Both themes of motherhood and «otherness» will be included and explored in *Medea* through a constant and intertwined opposition of languages.

In the moment when Scotland is starting to interrogate itself about the political and the cultural strategies to bring about independence and change, Euripides' concern about the changes undergone by his society and above all by women, his growing involvement in the female condition and his forerunning commitment to different «feminist» issues, become striking reference points to our Scottish writer. Greek tragedy, and Euripidean tragedy in particular, is indeed deeply concerned with problems and conflicts of gender. Euripides has in fact given voice to those usually silenced: to slaves, foreigners and women. And in no more play than *Medea* has Euripides presented such a powerful and subversive female character, and such a radical critique of male tradition and authority. *Medea* explores indeed the experience of an intelligent and self-determined woman in a society which denied women such attributes. She is an author and a voice, some sort of political hero, as she teaches us that even an outsider can change the world.

And even though in recent years feminist literary theory has seen the fifth-century tragedy as a tool of patriarchal repression, rather than as a way to subvert such male-driven ideology[88], the Greek trag-

---

[88] The way Aristophanes himself had addressed Euripides as «misogynist» was only a means to mock at him and offer a parodic reaction to his intense

edy in general, and *Medea*, in particular, is critical of established values and not at all supportive of women's prescribed roles of domesticity and ancillary silence. In fact, whether on the one hand Medea's imitation of a masculine code, her dehumanization and her betrayal of her own sex could confirm women's ultimate incapacity for independence and civilized behaviour and, in so doing, support feminist theories, on the other hand Medea shows women's oppression and their intelligence in a male-dominated society where such qualities are neglected and disallowed.

The repeated engagement with gender and the expected roles of men and women have been and remain issues of debate and potential conflict in most human communities, and above all in the Scottish one. The frequency of references in Greek plays to contemporary events and personalities, and thus to social, political and moral issues of the day - including all the irony and the humorous effects such references allow to intend - represents thus a big significant challenge to Liz Lochhead. She employs the myth as a model to depict and portray her own society, but never does it in a laudatory way, as writing about Scotland in the language of Scotland does not mean that everything has to be adulatory of Scottish culture.

«When I mentioned Clause 28» (Lochhead, 2000b, Intro)[89], she says, «I was just trying to say that to write from a dominantly Scottish perspective doesn't have to be celebratory of Scottish culture» (Pugliese, unpubl.). Scotland has in fact its own responsibility in its political weakness and, at the present, she is in danger of being destroyed by the Scots themselves.

---

portrayal of female condition and suffering (*Women at the Thesmophoria*, transl. Henderson, 2000: 372-465).

[89] In the Introduction to *Medea*, she mentioned Clause 28, also known as Section 28, of the Local Goverment Act 1988. It was a controversial amendment to the United Kingdom's Local Government Act 1986, enacted on 24 May 1988 and repealed on 21 June 2000 in Scotland, and on 18 November 2003 in the rest of the UK by section 122 of the of the Local Government Act 2003. The amendment stated that a local authority «shall not intentionally promote homosexuality or publish material with the intention of promoting homosexuality» or «promote the teaching in any maintained school of the acceptability of homosexuality as a pretended family relationship» (http://www.legislation.gov.uk/ukpga/1988/9/part/IV, last access 6th March, 2013).

The bigotry which has been exposed by the furore over the abolition of Clause 28 shows that we are a long way from a truly tolerant Scots society. The Athenian (male) society of his time which Euripides scourged for its smug and conventional attitudes of unthinking superiority to foreigners and women is unfortunately not totally unrecognisable, quaint or antique to me as I survey mine two and a half thousands years later. (Lochhead, 2000b, Intro)

«This macho Scottish culture» (Nicholson, 1992: 223), as Liz Lochhead had defined the Caledonian one, is still a limiting factor to women willing to participate into the social and political life. Regardless of the many repressive myths which continue to threaten Scottish society, and the patriarchal, Calvinist attitudes towards sexuality which still in the twenty-first century haunt Scotland, Scottish women should follow Medea's model and start speaking their own voices. Just like Medea, they should attempt to change their role from passive to active in the social contest and in so doing, establish their freedom and independence.

10. Medea: Probing into Independent Scots

Liz Lochhead's activity in employing vernacular starts with her masterpiece *Mary Queen of Scots got her Head chopped off* and proceeds with three main translations of classical plays: *Tartuffe, Thebans* and *Medea*. Since drama is the literary genre which best shows and practises the strength and vitality of language, and since Scots is a strangely theatrical language, Liz Lochhead's clever blending of Scots speech and theatre performance gives birth to some of the most brilliant plays in contemporary Scottish drama.

Unlike Burns and Scott, Liz Lochhead does not employ Scots as a means to mock and satirize common clichés she has been questioning ever since: in *Mary Queen of Scots got her Head Chopped Off* she uses the vernacular as a refined and highly crafted way of shaping characters and giving them insight. She explores Scots in the whole range of its dialects and registers and employs all the varieties of written and spoken Scots in the interest of political and social change. Her use of Scots reflects in social and local versatility, and all her characters speak a different language according to their social status and class position. The adaptations of the classical plays, instead, employ a different kind of Scots and reveal a gradually changing intention in using its potential. Lochhead's Scots is indeed a new and complex language, that develops and evolves from having sense only in its opposition to English towards a more striking use which reveals its mature independence in *Medea*.

In the version of Euripides' template, in fact, even though the problematic and unresolved relationship between Scotland and England is veiled under the continuous opposition between Scots and English, the certainty of English being the linguistic norm and of Scots the deviation from the norm - as it used to be in *Mary Queen of Scots Got Her Head Chopped Off* - is demystified and totally subverted. Whether in *Tartuffe* and *Thebans* Scots had in fact been employed as the language of the victims and the oppressed, in *Medea* its use is completely upturned and it now functions as an expression for civilized Greece. In the Introduction to the play the author explains her decision to make use of Scots and English in a new, unconventional way:

> It was only after seeing the play in performance [...] that it struck me the conventional way of doing Medea in Scotland until very recently would have been to have Medea's own language Scots and the, to her, alien Corinthians she lived under speaking, as powerful, «civilized» Greeks, patrician English. That it did not occur to me to do other than give the dominant mainstream society a Scots tongue and Medea a foreigner-speaking-English refugee voice must speak of a genuine in-the-bone increased cultural confidence here. (Lochhead, 2000b, Intro)

The unusual choice to have Medea speak English, rather than Scots, is further explained as an attempt to subvert the traditional colonial position that

> [Medea] was a foreigner and an outsider, so the conventional way to deal with such things would have been to accept a colonial position that the English was the dominant culture and to make her, maybe Scots, her language. Not to make her Scots, but to make her language Scottish in a dominantly English claim [...] She speaks fairly standard English, but a very strong foreign accent. She

has to speak English as a refugee or asylum seeker or something like that. [The other characters] speak Scots, but not incredibly strong Scots. It's not very difficult Scots. (Pugliese, unpubl.)

Scots is spoken by the mainstream society, whose «bigotry and conventional attitude of unthinking superiority to foreigners and women», would have conventionally been embodied by the «civilized», patrician English. And it is not at all a «literary Scots», but a demotic one - that is, the one spoken in the street, the colloquial urban Scots, and largely preferred in contemporary translations (Corbett, 1999: 180-183) - and here marked with a strong Glaswegian accent. In using demotic Scots as both a poetic and dramatic vehicle, Liz Lochhead has her language reflect politics and class: for this purpose, the often repeated words help shape her urban vernacular as real, as the language of the people, carrying the rhythms of «West-Scotland working-class experience into a form of social history» (Nicholson, 2007: 166).

In *Medea*, her language is not too experimental as she relies more on accent than on dialect to convey Scottishness to her characters. «The idiosyncratic quality of Lochhead's dramatic Scots lies partly in her ability to re-energise the clichés, catchphrases and slangy colloquialisms that she mentions in her introduction to *Tartuffe*» (Corbett, 2006: 27-28).

Nonetheless, since style and register switching are common in Scots dialects, Liz Lochhead's characters - from the King to the servant- incorporate stylistic shifts between accents and more or less standard options according to their social status, so that their linguistic behaviour changes with their class position.

> Their language varies from Scots to Scots-English, from time to time and from character to character – and particular emotional state of character. (Lochhead, 2000b: 3)

As noted by Corbett (2006), the socio-linguistic hierarchy of Lochhead's *Medea* is, however, visibly conservative: the grammar and vocabulary of the working classes are indeed less refined than the ones adopted by the ruling classes. Jason's idiom is in fact Scottish English, while the serving classes, as shown by the Manservant's following words, mix traditional Scots with contemporary slang:

MANSERVANT

madam the bairns are reprieved
they're safe   no banishment
I waited at the palace   watched
when my   lord Jason and the bairns came
back
we were over the moon
word wis among us slaves   the quarrel's
over
he was smiling the bride   thon Glauke
oor mistress in place of you   she
smiled too   picked up your wee lass
and sat her on her lap
hauding the bairns's wee hand against her
belly
whisperin that she'd feel her baby brother
kick
kissed her
than set her down again

(Lochhead, 2000b: 35)

At least, Kreon the King speaks now with a Scottish accent, since

> just because [he] is a king, he doesn't have to speak in
> Received Pronunciation English. (Pugliese, unpubl.)

Medea, even though with a strong foreign accent, is instead the only character who speaks English: by this means, her «otherness» as a woman and as a foreigner is linguistically marked as she now speaks English in a Scots-speaking society. The outcast, the foreigner Medea speaks «another» language which is not Scots and she is thus branded as an outsider by her own language.

English is no longer used as the oppressor's language, nor Scots as the language of the victims of history; Scots thus gains a much higher status and becomes the language of the dominant culture:

> Why shouldn't the dominant culture be Scots? It just de-
> pends on which language you decide to use as a *lingua*

franca. I decided to set the dominant culture as being Scots. It would have been a more colonial and colonized position to make the dominant culture English and have Scots informal. (Pugliese, unpubl.)

In employing Scots, it can be assumed that Liz Lochhead's main concern has been to look at Scotland through Scottish eyes: continuing a process started with Moliere's *Tartuffe*, she goes on giving importance and dignity to the sounds and rhythms of Scots, namely of urban Scots, as a cultural resistance to the dominance of English and to Received Pronunciation in British theatre.

For this purpose, the iambic trimeter employed by Euripides is abandoned, and rhythm is adopted as a more natural and musical way to convey meaning: namely, it replaces punctuation as a means of establishing sense.

Rhythm is oral and heard and free form. I didn't choose it: it came out. It was just to be very clear and enjoy the precision of the language. I loved the way that the Greek myths, in a certain sense, don't have any subtext. They are the subtext. (Pugliese, unpubl.)

Rhythm is nothing but pure poetry, written to be spoken loud. As a consequence, much of the play is written in short, staccato and half-lines. Sentences are short and often disjointed, words are repeated to stress meanings and emphasize tragic irony. Some language is extremely earthy in order to shape the text with real thoughts and feelings and, in so doing, remind the audience that these mythic archetypes are nothing more than normal human beings. In such a framework, Scots expressions can get higher resonance and therefore surpass meaning alone, in as much as dialect itself, being creative and effective in its striking solutions, intensifies the pathos.

Through the use of dialect and speech rhythms, which are typical features of the orality, Liz Lochhead replicates the musical unity of the original play. Through the rhythm of spoken Scots she shapes the sounds of the silenced voices. Her language is natural and straightforward, and nearly surpasses Euripides in brevity and directness. She often reduces the lines in extension, achieving in this way a more pungent and hitting effect without ever losing the sense of the original. Her language, though poetic, is much more crude and coarse than we might expect of the play and, yet, it never loses the sense of the grand political implications contained by the template.

Like Edwin Morgan, her use of vernacular is completely different from the one made by Young or Kemp[90]; she distances herself from classical Scots which previous writers had tried to fix and standard-ise, and invents a new one, «proverbial, slangy, couthy, clichéd, catch-phrasey and vulgar» (Lochhead, 1986, Intro). In fact, whereas Scottish Renaissance Lallans writers advocated Scots standardization, examples like Lochhead, Arnott and Morgan embody the opposite reaction to such a strong prescription and invent a new, and consist-ently different, language.

Against the fixed standard varieties, Liz Lochhead reinvents speech all the time and forges multiple varieties of stage Scots in order to be more effective on a verbal level for the Scottish audience. She exploits the combination and the opposition of Scots and Eng-lish as more effective than Standard English alone in rendering the spirit and the tones of the template. «Wonderful though the English language is» (Findlay, 1996: 204), it offers less range than dialect and «as a translation medium, it can have a homogenising effect on for-eign work» (IVI).

In rewriting the source play for the contemporary stage, Liz Lochhead's Scots translation both reaches the contemporary specta-tor and honours the source it is adapting.

11. The Bride and the Mother

Suddenly there's the me in the mirror staring back at me and me less than amazed at me all marcelled like Elsa Lanchester. Well, it's apt enough, this is my last morning as a single girl. [...] And because last night was my last night, last night I left you, left you to your own devices under our double duvet, left home and went home, home to Home home, to sleep my last night in my old single bed. [...] And here's the taxi and I stretch up my arms like one beseeching heaven, I stretch my arms like one embracing fate and four sets of arms help me into my dress, my dress I don't want to wear, my dress that after the whole caffuffle is

---

[90] Like Morgan, Liz Lochhead extends oral forms towards the written regis-ter of literature starting from an urban base, and not from a rural one like Young and Kemp. Nonetheless, her demotic Scots is very different from Morgan's, even though each is coloured by the other. Along with Loch-head's *Tartuffe*, Edwin Morgan's *Cyrano de Bergerac* (1992) has been a pioneer-ing work in the regard of Scots adaptations.

really nothing special, my dress that should you jilt me, leave me in the lurch at
the altar of the registry office, tilting my fragile psyche for ever permanently agley,
the dress I'll have to wear as a penance till I'm dafter than Miss Havisham, in
mourning for my life until it rots under the oxters. I should've chosen very careful-
ly. [...]We scorn such sentimental institutionalizing as making love on this our
wedding night, and it's only after [...] practised and perfect we judder totally
together into amazed and wide-eyed calm and I lie beside you utterly content. I
know for sure that this is never ever going to work.

(Liz Lochhead, *The Bride*, 1991)

In the introduction to the play, Liz Lochhead states that when Graham McLaren approached her about doing a version of *Medea* she
was writing a comedy about a woman desperate to give birth to a
child, and the idea of working on exactly the opposite, namely on a
play about a woman killing her own children, was a kind of «perverse
attraction» (Lochhead, 2000b, Intro) which actually made her accept.
«It's nice to do the opposite things» (Pugliese, unpubl.), she says.
While working on the text, though, such a stimulus soon evolved in
the growing interest in

> looking for what dramatic forces [were there]. While I
> was reading [the many English translations of Euripides'
> *Medea*], I picked and chose, to try and get an essence of
> the *pièce*. For me it [was] just literally making every bit of
> it. Feel true to human beings. I wasn't particularly inter-
> ested in her as a literal goddess or a literal sorcerer. I was
> interested in her human aspects. [...] I didn't set out to
> be different from the original. I was just trying to find
> the deep truth in what I see there. (Pugliese, unpubl.)

The involvement in rewriting old myths and literary archetypes
which, as already stated, permeates Liz Lochhead's whole production, stands alongside with her continuing interest in writing about
female concerns, motherhood being the most striking of them. The
constraining myth of motherhood is indeed probed both as an act of
creation and as a cultural construct since the very beginning of her
writing activity.

Medea is a mother because and as long as she is a bride. Motherhood is a feminine stance already inspected by Liz Lochhead in *Blood*
and Ice, where the dilemma of woman as mother and as artist have

been associated and questioned. In this play, in fact, she had tackled and demystified the myth of problematic motherhood, and exposed this idea of femininity as a product of male imagination that forces upon women a double and challenging perception of themselves.

Exposed to the risks of childbearing and childbirth, and often dependent on fathers, brothers or husbands, women have always been biologically and socially disadvantaged. All Athenian women, regardless of their socio-economic class, were in fact marginal members of the πόλις, since they had no role in its public and political life. Against this lack of power and self-determination was instead set their important role as mothers and bearers of the male citizen-soldier who would ensure security and survival to the city[91].

Unfortunately, this is particularly true in Scotland and above all among working-class communities where women, often due to extreme poverty, still suffer from the restrictions of a fundamentally patriarchal society and undergo social and political changes at a slow pace. Women have always been intended as perfect wives and mothers, looking after the house and bringing up children. They used to have neither properties nor jobs, and in such a context, their personal autonomy and intellectual development were reduced to none. Medea has little resemblance to such women: she is the equal of man, in both intelligence and courage, creativity and independence. Medea has in fact made clear that marriage is everything to a woman and that she thinks of herself as a woman and is thought by others as a woman. When the play opens, though, Medea is no longer a wife, and when it closes she is no longer a mother. She is something more: a demon of revenge, a goddess or a monster, who has given up her humanity and killed her own children[92]. She raises herself up, out of the world. She is all things between heaven and earth: she is lion, rock, *daimon*, fury, a free spirit. She is something not human: subhuman or superhuman, it is hardly relevant.

Even though Euripides' Medea felt and claimed her children as her own, she knew that they were not really hers, as they belonged to Jason. She thus killed them because they were the most important

---

[91] Furthermore, the new citizenship law proposed by Pericles in 451 BC decreed that a man could only be a citizen if both his parents were Athenians. Athenian women became thus essential to the community, in as much as they would guarantee the community legitimate heirs.

[92] She repeatedly says she is the grandchild of the Sun god, and in so doing she asserts her divine lineage and her semi-goddess nature.

thing to him and the only one worth being sacrificed to fulfil her revenge against him. She has been neglected as a woman in as much as she had been refused as a wife, and she now thus takes her revenge as a woman hitting Jason as a male, husband and citizen, on his dearest property: his offspring. Liz Lochhead's Medea on the contrary knows that her children are only hers and that she is the only one responsible for them and their destiny. And even though the choice she is going to make is so cruel and unnatural, she is the only one endowed with the possibility to decide on their behalf.

12. Medea: An Ideal Woman?

> *But my wrath overbears my calculation, wrath*
> *that brings mortal men their gravest hurt*

> (*Medea* 1079-80, transl. Kovacs, 1994)

In Liz Lochhead's version Medea's supernatural nature is diminished and nearly annulled, in order to have her human sufferings achieve much higher resonance and introspection. Medea's feelings and choices, her thoughts and fears are indeed highlighted as totally human and thus tragically dividing. She is now entirely mortal and her courage and resolution do not make her out of the world, but do make her voice heard in the contemporary world.

She is at the edge, but she shows what we are. She is a woman among women. She is an incredible portrait of a soul scourged by fate, and her suffering is primal and extreme. She stands for the «new» woman, the brave one, whose freedom of thought and action has been claimed by many Scottish contemporary women now more vigorously than ever. Liz Lochhead says about her:

> My Medea is not supernatural, not an immortal, but is all too human. Even if she does have some spectacular poisons and skills I chose not to interpret them as spells. The mixed marriage between Jason and Medea isn't between a man and a demi-goddess, but between a man and a woman. (Lochhead, 2000b, Intro)

Moreover, Medea is a «pantomime dame dignified, sexualized and made into the tragic centre of the play» (Corbett, 2006: 30), and this makes her more human - and monstrous- than ever.

> tigress? fury? harpy? witch? she wolf?
> monster? yes, I am!
> for I have torn out your heart and devoured it
>
> (Lochhead, 2000b: 45)

With her strong emotions and extreme vindictiveness «she retains some elements of the pantomime dame» (Corbett, 2006, p. 30). She kills her children to show Jason what it means to be human and to live as a human being. She wants her children to die, because they will have more value if they are dead; at the same time, her deed will ensure her the prominence she had never been recognised.

Through infanticide she surpasses her mortal attributes and thus joins the mythic dimension. She is not an extraordinary creature whose stunning skills and miraculous poisons are spells leading her towards the horrible deed, but a human being - a woman in particular- who can now speak out to the world her revenge and take responsibility for it. It is only after having killed her children that she surpasses her all human essence and finally enters the supernatural dimension:

> I think extreme deeds do take you into the mythic dimension. If you join the place called «myth», you are a sort of immortal, you are like a god. (Pugliese, unpubl.)

When Medea accepts Aegeus proposal, she decides to be a wife again. She will in fact have a city and a home, and perhaps, at some point, she will bear a royal son, as she had promised, to the man who rescued her. She will hence have achieved what, according to Jason, she was lacking - namely, a royal child, royal patronage and conspicuous glory. She will live with the King of Athens in a reciprocal relationship in which what she has to offer is really appreciated and eventually valued.

> For myself, I shall go to Erechtheus' land, to share the home of Aegeus, son of Pandion. (Euripides, *Medea*. 1384-5, transl. J. Davie, 2003)

Medea stands uncorrupted and is something of a redemptive figure for all women mistreated in marriage and silenced by men. She has to remain that brave and determined woman whose voice as a hero is now spoken and heard.

In retelling some specific myths rather than others, the Scottish playwrights and their publishers have certainly felt a political or aesthetic affinity with the cultures whose source texts they have chosen to translate and adapt. They might also have been attracted by some established cultural ideas they wanted to fit, or, on the other hand, they only wanted to introduce a new concept they felt the Scottish culture is lacking.

In adapting *Medea*, Liz Lochhead manipulates the classical myth in accordance with the developments of Scottish political culture and at the same to explore the new potentialities of theatre in Scots. Her main concern is to follow Graham McLaren's suggestion and extend the range of the Scots idiom as well as contribute to the reborn Scottish theatre tradition. The myth, which is used as a source of generally acknowledged values and universal meanings, is applicable to every culture.

Liz Lochhead invites her audience not only to listen to her Scottish voice, but to identify with it, detect common ground and actively empathize with the hi-story presented. Through *Medea*, she retells the myth in order to both contribute to Scottish literature, and enhance national political awareness. In so doing, Scotland's «daurk forest» is explored and depicted, while the universal power of myth is again asserted and renewed.

> I couldn't do Medea without her being a woman and as disconcerting a figure as she is to Euripides. [...] Greek plays are about the human condition. She is contemporary and ancient as well. She will always be contemporary as long as we are human beings. (Pugliese, unpubl.)

CONCLUSIONS 🪷

Religious symbols, myth and ritual, in which the theme of sacrifice plays a fundamental role, are examples of the defensive, protective strategies with which the community helps release the fury and, through the repeated foundation and affirmation of a cultural system, prepares the way for the assertion of a value. In fifth-century Athens, where women still had no legal status and very little public role either, the social crisis that clearly affected the female world most forcibly found release through a Maenadism that often had to be confined to the ahistorical dimension of myth. Only in myth was it possible to overturn the traditional values of the *polis* and reject its rules; and only in myth and ritual was this subversion entrusted to symbolic models of representation that in the timeless sphere of myth served to exorcize the real and guarantee a return to the customary order.

Child-killing in classical myth was therefore part of a symbolic and prevalently mythical creative response to the crisis, which was above all individual and prevalently female. In a desacralized world like ours, however, where myth and ritual have lost their primary stabilizing functions, man is unable to find satisfactory models of cultural resolution and so becomes easy prey to existential anguish and re-establishes order, not through imagined forms of release, but through confused scenarios of oppression and destruction.

For some time now a dark nihilism, a sinister longing for a twilight of the gods has been spreading in the modern world as a force that cannot find sufficient models of cultural resolution or socially acceptable channels for releasing or containing that are morally reconcilable with the knowledge of human values that has been laboriously achieved in thousands of years of history in the West[93].

---

[93] (Orig.): «É da tempo che una cupa invidia del nulla, una sinistra tentazione da crepuscolo degli dei dilaga nel mondo moderno come una forza che non trova adeguati modelli di risoluzione culturale, e che non si disciplina in un alveo di deflusso e di arginamento socialmente accettabile e moralmente conciliabile con la coscienza dei valori umani faticosamente

At the mercy of a terrible death instinct and a Freudian longing for nothingness, modern man deludes himself that he can solve any crisis through chaotic and destructive behavior in which all his rage is vented in a regressive tendency that is never placated. The field of mythical speech gives way to that of sacrificial action, no longer as part of the symbolic framework of ritual, but embodied in the reality of daily life.

In closing, it may be worth offering some quick thoughts that might, with an eye to (one hopes) possible future work on this subject, involve further theoretical and methodological considerations. The two texts discussed, with their significant differences, have been presented as the results of a rewriting of Euripides' hypotext or of the underlying myth of Medea. Strictly speaking, if by rewriting we mean a strictly literary operation in which an author directly retrieves a text to set it on the same plane of discourse, the present work would lose its *raison d'être*. In fact, the reworkings chosen have been taken as cultural documents that can be set in a substantially autonomous frame work, whose fertile recodification of the mythological material defines each time the relation between literature and mythology on different ethno-anthropological premises.

In literary criticism, the post-modern period has seen the development of a considerable number of trends, all sharing the same label of post-structuralism and the aim of abandoning the structuralist project of defining literary qualities scientifically. This is the scenario that explains the inclusion of Liz Lockhead's *Medea* as a work of translation and cultural transposition, and Toni Morrison's novel, in which the mythologem is only latently and allusively present and the variation on the character is part of the text's aim to reject the model and to offer a new hermeneutic reference.

Although thematic criticism is inherently anti-systematic in its definitions, orientations and interpretative methods, it has been a fixed landmark on the historical-critical and cultural scene in recent years. Its strength seems to lie precisely in its escaping rigid, prescriptive schemas, and so lending itself to various premises and objectives. Its frequent combining with «other» disciplines continues to encourage the study of the specific imaginative world of given ethnic groups and social categories, as well as an interdisciplinary approach.

---

conquistata nel corso della millenaria storia d'Occidente». (De Martino, 2002: 173-171).

The pleasure of repetition and mimicry are both inscribed in the psychic and cultural dynamics of man, and the explicit reworking of a text, or simply referring to it more or less directly, becomes for the two writers examined the creation of a narrative and poetological space that is essentially independent. Although the reader is expected to be familiar with the original text, the reworking is sufficiently autonomous not to require a direct comparison with it to be understood, leaving the contemporary author all sorts of ways of rewriting it. The myth contains a set of constants and variants that change with the changing historical-cultural contexts. For the Greek world the clash and confrontation with other populations had been an important means for constructing their own identity. Similarly, during the twentieth century, reflection on the relation with the other became particularly deep-felt, partly due to the combined effects of many other cultural factors, such as anthropology, post-colonial criticism and psychoanalysis, which enormously extended the range of literary theory. Based mainly on the thematic nucleus of barbarism and alterity, the myth of Medea in the twentieth century was represented in a new light with a positive connotation: the two twentieth-century rewritings of the myth reached very different results, but shared the same desire to identify themselves with Medea's ethnic and cultural diversity so as to rethink critically her and her story.

Medea's story, taken as representing the conflicts and problems of the most various cultures and minority ethnic groups, continues to find the most varied expressions in different artistic fields, from theatre to melodrama, from the novel to the cinema, the figurative and plastic arts, confirming its extraordinary vitality in the present-day artistic scene. The thematic nucleus of the foreigner's diversity and the difficulty of relationships is still the aspect of the myth that is most frequently taken up in recent works of art. If we limit ourselves to Italian works – and take the opportunity to make them better known abroad – we might recall the most interesting new play of 2004, which was Emma Dante's rewriting of it, in which the various dramatic innovations serve to debunk every aspect of the myth. Set in a small village of the South, the story revolves around a priest-father, an obese king and five sterile women who are paradoxically played by a chorus of men, who represent a male population unsuitable for receiving and developing the seed. Jason is king of a sterile city, while Medea, imagined as pregnant after giving birth to her children, ends the play by drowning them in the font.

Another Italian reworking in the first decade of the new millennium was that by Gianluca Bottoni, whose *Olà Medea!* (2008) offers a new twist to the story: Medea is a trans-sexual who has only recently become a woman, and lives out to the full the tragedy of diversity and not belonging, *in primis* to herself and her own body. Aegeus is an impotent king who can have children only in the test-tube, while Medea, whose diversity now means that, for the first time in the myth, she cannot become a mother, and thanks to this biological limit no longer kills her children and remains faithful to the values of the maternity she believes in. Her salvation comes about through her awareness of the co-existence of infinite natural mutations of forms, which equally confirm the centrality of the metamorphosis of the character in the dynamics of the story.

Another example is provided by the Trieste composer Davide Casali, who in 2009 made a film entitled *Medea fuori del mito (Medea out of the Myth)*, which was clearly intended from the outset to break with tradition. The story is reconstructed by the protagonist, who tells her story in the first person. After falling in love with Jason, Medea leaves for Greece with him, where, after receiving the blessing of her parents, she enjoys a quiet life and the affection of her children and husband. Soon, however, the whole story proves to be simply a wish-fulfillment fantasy of Medea's, and the author insinuates the doubt that the infanticide was caused merely by the Greeks misunderstanding her words and actions. Once again, the story of the foreign Medea proves to be highly topical in a society that, thousands of years later, is more and more wounded by xenophobic and racist attitudes.

The process of creatively reworking the myth of Medea as a way of analyzing significant aspects of contemporary cultural life is, then, widespread and deep-rooted in contemporary art, and certainly offers further possibilities for future research into its many implications. Medea's popularity is also due to all those writers who, in all periods and cultures, have parodied, imitated, reworked or repudiated Euripides' masterpiece.

REFERENCES ❧

ADAMI ROOK P., (1983) *Le due Femminilità: la crisi della coscienza femminile nel sogno e nel mito*, Roma, Bulzoni

ARISTOPHANES (republ. 2000) *Women at the Thesmophoria*, (transl. J. Henderson) Loeb Classical Library, 179, Cambridge, Harvard University Press: 372-465

ASTON, E., (1995) *An introduction to Feminism and Theatre*, London and New York, Routledge

BACHTIN, M., (1973) *Voprosy literatury i estetiki* (it. transl.) (1979) *Estetica e Romanzo*, Torino, Einaudi: 445-482

BACHOFEN, J.J., (1967) *Mother Right*, Princeton, N.J., Princeton University Press (orig.1861)

BARTHES, R., (1972) *Mythologies,* (transl. A. Lavers), London, Jonathan Cape

BASSNETT, S., (2002) *Translation Studies*, London, Routledge

BELL, B., (1987) *The Afro-American Novel and its Tradition*, Amherst, University of Massachusetts Press

BELTRAMETTI, A., (2000) *Eros e maternità. Quel che resta del conflitto tragico di Medea*, in Gentili, B., Perusino, F., (eds.), *Medea nell'Arte e nella Letteratura*, Vicenza, Marsilio: 43-65

BENJAMIN, J., (1988) *The Bonds of Love: Psychoanalysis, Feminism, and the Problem of Domination.* London, Virago

BERNAL, M., (1987) *Black Athena: the Afroasiatic Roots of Classical Civilization.* Vol. 1, *The Fabrication of Ancient Greece 1785-1985.* New Brunswick, N.J., Rutgers University Press

— ID. (1991) *Black Athena: the Afroasiatic Roots of Classical Civilization.* Vol. 2, *Archaeological and Documentary Evidence.* New Brunswick, N.J., Rutgers University Press

BERLINERBLAU, J., (1999) *Heresy in the University: The Black Athena Controversy and the Responsibilities of American Intellectuals.* New Brunswick, N.J., Rutgers University Press

BLUMENBERG, H., (1991), *L'elaborazione del Mito*, Bologna, Il Mulino, (orig. 1979) *Arbeit am Mythos*

BRENKMAN, J., (1992) «Family, Community, Polis: The Freudian Structure of Feeling» in *New Literary History*, 23: 923-54

BRAUN, A.K., (2004) *Dramatic Laboratories. Figurations of Subjectivity on Liz Lochhead's Writings*, Berlin, Galda Wilch Verlag

— EAD. (2006) *Resignifying HiStories: The Subversive Potential of Revision in Liz Lochhead's Poetry*, in *Ethically Speaking. Voice and Values in Modern Scottish Writing*, McGonigal, J. – Stirling, K., (eds.) Amsterdam-New York, Radopi: 69-85

Brown I., (2007) *Staging the Nation: Multiplicity and Cultural Diversity in Contemporary Scottish Theatre*, in Ibid. (eds.) *The Edinburgh History of Scottish Literature* (vol.3): *Modern transformations: New Identities (from 1918)*, Edinburgh, Edinburgh University Press: 283-294

Butler, J., (1990a) *Performative Acts and Gender Constitution: An Essay in Phenomenology and Feminist Theory*, in Case S.E. (eds.) *Performing Feminism: Feminist Critical Theory and Theatre*, Baltimore and London, The John Hopkins UP, 1990: 270-282

— EAD. (1990b) *Gender Trouble. Feminism and the Subversion of Identity*, New York: Routledge

— EAD. (1993) *Bodies that Matter: on the Discursive Limits of Sex*, New York, Routledge

Buschendorf, C., (1997) «White Masks: Greek Mythology in Contemporary Black Poetry», *Crossing Border: Inner-and Intercultural Exchanges in a Multicultural Society*, (eds.), Heinz Ickstadt, Germany, Peter Lang: 65-82

Carotenuto, A., (1978) *Psiche e Inconscio*, Venezia, Marsilio

— ID. (1991) *Trattato di Psicologia della Personalità*, Milano, Raffaello Cortina Editore

— ID. (2001) *L'Anima delle Donne*, Milano, Bompiani

Ceserani, R., (1998) *Lo Straniero*, Roma-Bari, Laterza

— ID. e Domenichelli, M. - Fasano, P., (2007) *Dizionario dei temi letterari, 3 voll.* Torino: UTET

— ID. (2010) *Convergenze. Gli strumenti letterari e le altre discipline*, Milano, Mondadori

Christianson, A., (2000) *Liz Lochhead's Poetry and Drama: Forging Ironies*, in Ibid. *Contemporary Scottish Women Writers*, Edinburgh, Edinburgh University Press

Cixous, H., (1975) (transl. K. and P. Cohen), *The Laugh of the Medusa*, Signs: 1.4 (1976): 875-93

Clauss J.J.- Johnston, S.I. (eds.) (1997) *Medea. Essays on Medea in Myth, Literature, Philosophy and Art*, Princeton N.J., Princeton University Press

Corbett J., (1997) *Language and Scottish Literature*, Edinburgh, Edinburgh University Press

— ID. (1999) *Written in the Language of the Scottish Nation. A History of Literary Translation into Scots*, Clavendon, Multilingual Matters Ltd

— ID. and Findlay, B. (eds.) (2005) *Serving Twa Maisters. Five Classics Plays in Scots Translations*, Glasgow, Bell & Bain

— ID. (2006) «*Nae mair pussyfootin. Ah'm aff, Theramenes*»: *Demotic Neoclassical Drama in Contemporary Scotland*, in McGonigal, J. – Stirling, K. (eds.) *Ethically Speaking. Voice and Values in Modern Scottish Writing*, Amsterdam-New York, Radopi, 2006: 17-35

— ID. (2007) *A Double Realm: Scottish Literary Translation in the Twenty-first Century*, in Schoene, B. (eds.) *The Edinburgh Companion to Contemporary Scottish Literature*, Edinburgh, Edinburgh University Press, 2007: 336-344

CORTI L., (1988) *The Myth of Medea and Murder of Children*, Westport, CT, Greenwood Press

— EAD. (1992) «Medea and Beloved: Self-Definition and Abortive Nurturing in Literary Treatments of the Infanticidal Mother», *Disorderly Eaters; Texts in Self-Empowerment*, (eds.) Lillian R. Furst and Peter W. Graham. Pennsylvania, Pennsylvania University Press: 61-77

CRAIG, C., (1996) *From the lost Ground: Liz Lochhead, Douglas Dunn, and Contemporary Scottish Poetry*, in Acheson, J. and Huk R. (eds.) *Contemporary British Poetry*, Albany, NY, State University of New York Press: 343-372

— ID. (2001) and STEVENSON, R. (eds.) *Twentieth Century Scottish Drama*, Edinburgh, Canongate

CRAIGIE, W.A. et al., (eds.) (1925-2002) *DOST, Dictionary of the Older Scottish tongue* (12 vols) London, Oxford University Press

CRAWFORD, R., (1992) *Devolving English Literature*, Edinburgh, Edinburgh University Press

CURTI, L., (2006) *La Voce dell'Altra*, Roma, Meltemi

DELEUZE, G., (republ. 2001) *Difference and Repetition*, London and New York, Continuum (Orig. 1968)

DENHOLM, R.M., (eds.), (1953) *The Scottish National Theatre Venture*, Glasgow, Scottish National Players

DE WEEVER, J, (1991) *Mythmaking and Metaphor in Black Women's Fiction*. New York, St. Martin's Press

DURRANT, S., (2004) *Postcolonial Narrative and the Work of Mourning*, New York, State University of New York Press

ELIADE, M., (1958) (orig. 1949) *Patterns in comparative Religions*, (transl. R. Sheed), London, Sheed and Ward

— (republ. 1997), *Images and Symbols: Studies in Religious Symbolism*, Princeton N.J., Princeton University Press

ELIOT, T.S. (1922) *Tradition and the individual Talent*, in *The sacred Wood: essays on poetry and criticism*, London, Methuen &co

EURIPIDES, (trans. Philip Vellacott) (1968) *Medea and Other Plays*, London, Penguin Harmondsworth

— ID. (transl. D. Kovacs) (1994) *Medea*, London, Harvard University Press

— ID. (transl. J. Davie) (2003) Medea, London, Penguin

FINDLAY, B., (1996) *Translating into Dialect*, in Johnston, D. (eds.) *Stages in Translation*, Bath: Absolute Press: 199-217

— ID. (eds.) (1998) *A History of Scottish Theatre*, Edinburgh, Polygon

— ID. (2000) *Translating standard into Dialect: Missing the target?* in Upton, C.A. (eds.) *Moving Target: Theatre Translation and Cultural Relocation*, Manchester, St. Jerome: 35-46

— ID. (eds.) (2004) *Frae Ither Tongues, Essays on Modern Translations into Scots*, Clavendon, Multilingual Matters Ltd

FIUME, G., (1995) *Madri. Storia di un ruolo sociale*, Venezia, Marsilio

FOLEY, H.P., (2001) *Female Acts in Greek Tragedy*, Princeton, N.J., Princeton University Press

FREUD, S., (1905) *Three Essays on the Theory of Sexuality*, The Standard Edition of the Complete Works of Sigmund Freud, 24 volumes, (1953-74) James Strachey et al. (eds.), London, The Hogarth Press and the Institute of Psychoanalysis, 7: 125-245

— ID. (1912) *On the Universal Tendency to Debasement in the Sphere of Love*, SE 11: 179-190

— ID. (1913) *Totem and Taboo*, SE 13: 1-161

— ID. (1914) *On Narcissism: An Introduction*, SE 14: 67-102

— ID. (1918) *The Taboo of Virginity*, SE 11: 191-208

— ID. (1925) *Some Psychical Consequences of the Anatomical Distinction between the Sexes*. SE 19: 241-258

FRYE, N., (1967) «Literature and Myth.» *Relations of Literary Study: Essays in Interdisciplinary Contributions*, (eds.) James Thorpe. New York, MLA: 27-55

— ID. (1969) *Cultura e Miti del nostro Tempo*, Milano, Rizzoli

— ID. (1973) *Favole di Identità, Studi di Mitologia Poetica*, Torino, Einaudi

FUSILLO, M., (1998) *L'altro e lo stesso. Teoria e storia del doppio*, Scandicci, La Nuova Italia

— ID. (2009) *Estetica della Letteratura*, Bologna, Il Mulino

GALLOWAY, J. (eds.) (1991) *Meantime: Looking forward to the Millennium – An Anthology of Women's Writing*, Edinburgh, Polygon

GENETTE, G., (1997) *Palimpsests: Literature in the Second Degree*, (transl. C. Newman- C. Doubinsky), Lincoln, University of Nebraska Press

GENTILI, B., PERUSINO, F., (eds.), (2000) *Medea nell'Arte e nella Letteratura*, Venezia, Marsilio

GIFFORD, D., et al. (eds.) (2002) *Scottish Literature in English and Scots*, Edinburgh, Edinburgh University Press

GIGLIOLI, D., (2000) *Tema*, Firenze, La Nuova Italia

GIRARD, R. (1977) *Violence and the Sacred*, (transl. P. Gregory), Baltimore, Johns Hopkins University Press (orig. 1972, *La Violence et le Sacré*)

— ID. (1986) *The Scapegoat*, Baltimore, The Johns Hopkins University Press (orig. 1982, *Le Bouc émissaire*)

GREIG, D., (2005) *Oedipus the Visionary*, Edinburgh, Capercaillie Books

GOFF, B.- SIMPSON, M., (2007) *Crossroads in the Black Aegean; Oedipus, Antigone, and Dramas of the African Diaspora*. Oxford, Oxford University Press

GONZALES, C.R., «An Interview with Liz Lochhead», *ATLANTIS* 26.1 (June 2004): 101-110

GRAVES RANKE, R., (1983) *I miti greci*, Milano, Longanesi, (orig. 1954)

GREENWOOD, E., (2009) «Re-rooting the Classical Tradition: New Directions in Black Classicism». *Classical Reception Journal*, Vol. 1 Iss. I: 87-103

GREWAL, G., (2000) *Circles of Sorrow, Lines of Struggle. The Novels of Toni Morrison*, Lousiana University Press

GUASTELLA, G., (2000) «*Il Destino dei Figli di Giasone*». Medea nell'Arte e nella Letteratura, (eds.) B. Gentili e F. Perusino, Venezia, Marsilio

GUTHRIE, T., (1994) *Conversations with Toni Morrison*. Mississippi, University Press of Mississippi

HALEY, S., (1993) «Black Feminist Thought and Classics: Re-membering Reclaiming, Re-empowering». *Feminist Theory and the Classics*, (eds.) Nancy Sorkin Rabinowitz and Amy Richlin. New York, Routledge: 23-43

— EAD. (1995) «Self Definition, Community and Resistance. Euripides' *Medea* and Toni Morrison's *Beloved*». *Thamyris: Mythmaking from Past to Present 2*: 177-206

HALL, E., (2000) Medea in Performance 1500-2000, Oxford, European Humanities Research Centre

HARDICK, L., (2000) Translating Words, Translating Cultures, London, Duckworth

— EAD. (2003) *Reception Studies,* n.33, Oxford, Oxford University Press

HARROWER, D. – GRIEG, D., (Scotsman, 25 November 1997) Why a new Scotland mush have a properly-funded theatre

HENDRY, J., (1989) *Twentieth-century Women's Writing: The Nest of Singing Birds*, in Craig, C. (eds.) *The History of Scottish Literature*, vol.4, *The Twentieth Century*, Aberdeen, Aberdeen University Press: 291-309

HOESTEREY, I., (2001) *Pastiche. Cultural Memory in Art, Film, Literature*, Boomington-Indianapolis, Indiana University Press, cap. I

HUTCHEON, L., (1985) *A theory of parody. The Teachings of Twentieth-Century Art Forms,* New York, Methuen

— EAD. (1988) *A Poetics of Postmodernim,. History, Teory, Fiction*, New York-London, Routledge

HUTCHISON, D., (1977) *The Modern Scottish Theatre*, Glasgow, Molendinar Press

— ID. (1987) *Scottish Drama 1900-1950*, in Craig, C. (eds.) *The History of Scottish Literature*, (vol.4): *The Twelfth Century*, Aberdeen, Aberdeen University Press: 163-177

HYPPOCRATES, (2012) *On the Nature of the Child*, Cambridge, LCL Harvard university Press

IRIGARAY, L., (1985) *Speculum of the Other Woman*. New York, Cornell University Press (orig. 1974)

JONES, W., - VINSON, A., (1985) «An Interview qwith Toni Morrison», in in *Conversations with Toni Morrison*, (eds.), Danielle Taylor- Guthrye, (1994) Mississippi, University Press of Mississippi: 171-187

JUNG, K.G., (1956) *Symbols of Transformation*, Collected Works vol. 24, Volume 5, Princeton, N.J., Princeton University Press (orig. 1912)

— ID. (1966) *Two Essays on Analytical Psychology*, Princeton, N.J., Princeton University Press

— ID. (1981) *Archetypes and the Collective Unconscious*, (eds. and transl. G. Adler and R.F.C. Hull) Collected Works, vol. 24, Vol. 9 Part 1, Princeton N.J., Princeton University Press

KERENYI, K., - C.G. JUNG (republ. 1969) *Essays on a Science of Mythology* Princeton, N.J., Princeton University Press

KLEIN, M., (1957) *Envy and gratitude: A study of unconscious forces (The writings of Melanie Klein*, Vol. 3), London, Hogarth Press

— EAD. (republ. 1975a) *Love, Guilt and Reparation (The Writings of Melanie Klein*, Vol.1), London, Hogarth Press

— EAD. (republ. 1975b) *The Psycho-Analysis of Children (The Writings of Melanie Klein*, Vol.2), London, Hogarth Press (orig. 1932)

KRISTEVA, J., (1980) *Desire in Language: A Semiotic Approach to Literature and Art*, Oxford, Blackwell (orig. 1969)

LACEY, W.K., (1968) *The Family in classical Greece*, Ithaca-New York

LE FANU, J. S., (2000) *Carmilla*, London, Penguin Books

LEFKOWITZ, M. R., (1992) «Not Out of Africa: The Origins of Greece and the Illusions of Afrocentrists». *New Republic* (10 Febbraio): 29-36

— EAD. and Guy ROGERS, (1996) *Black Athena Revisited*. Chapel Hill, University of North Carolina Press

LOCHHEAD, L., (1972) *Memo for Spring* in EAD. (1984) *Dreaming Frankenstein & Collected Poems*, Edinburgh: Polygon

— EAD. (1981) *The Grimm Sisters* in EAD. (1984) *Dreaming Frankenstein & Collected Poems*, Edinburgh: Polygon

— EAD. (1985a) *Blood and Ice*, in *Plays by Women*, (vol 4), (selected and introduced by Wandor, M.), London and New York, Routledge, 1985a: 81-118

— EAD. (1985b) *True Confessions and New Clichès*, Edinburgh, Polygon

— EAD. (1986) *Tartuffe. A Translation into Scots from the Original by Molière*, Edinburgh, Polygon

— EAD. (1989) *Mary Queen of Scots got her head chopped off* and *Dracula*, London, Penguin

— EAD. (1998) *Mirror's Song*, in *Three Scottish Poets*, London, Canongate Classics

— EAD. (1991a) *Bagpipe Muzak*, London, Penguin

— EAD. (1991b) *Womens' Writing and the Millennium. Meantime: Looking Forward to the Millennium. An Anthology of Women's Writing*, (Introduced by Galloway, J.), Edinburgh, Polygon: 69-75

— EAD. (2000a) *Dreaming Frankenstein & Collected Poems*, Edinburgh, Polygon

— EAD. (2000b) *Medea after Euripides*, London, Nick Hern Books

— EAD. (2004) *Thebans, after Sophocles and Euripides*, London, Nick Herns Books

LUPERINI; R., (2005), *La fine del Postmoderno*, Napoli, Guida

LUSHING, C.A.E., (2007) *Granddaughter of the Sun: A Study of Euripides' Medea*, Leiden-Boston, Brill

MACDOUGALL, C., (2004) *Writing Scotland: How Scotland's Writers Shaped the Nation*, Edinburgh, Polygon

MANZONI. A., (2006) *I Promessi Sposi*, Milano, I Meridiani, (orig. 1827)

MCCLURE, J. D., (2000) *Language, Poetry and Nationhood: Scots as a Poetic Language from 1878 to the Present*, East Linton, Tuckwell Press

MCDONALD, J., (1997) Scottish Women Dramatists since 1945, in Gifford, D.- McMillan, D., (eds.) A History of Scottish Women's Writing, Edinburgh, Edinburgh University Press, 1997: 494-513

MCGRATH, T., (2005) *Electra*, Edinburgh, Capercaillie Books

MATTE BLANCO I., (1975) *The Unconscious as Infinite Sets*, London, Karnac

MILDONIAN, P. (eds.) (1997) *Parodia, Pastiche e Mimetismo*, Roma, Bulzoni

MORGAN, E., (1990) Crossing the Border: Essays on Scottish Literature, Manchester, Carcanet

— ID. (1992) *Edmond Rostand's Cyrano de Bergerac*, Manchester, Carcanet

— ID. (1996) *Collected Translations*, Manchester, Carcanet

— ID. (2000) *Jean Racine's Phaedra: A Tragedy*, Manchester, Carcanet

MORINI, M., (2005) Liz Lochhead's Poetry and Dram: In Her Own Voice?, in Fazzini, M., Alba Literaria. A History of Scottish Literature, Venezia, Amos Edizioni: 687-700

MORRISON, T., (Cloe Ardellia Wofford), (1983) «Virginia Woolf's and William Faulkner's Treatment of the Alienated». M.A. Thesis, Cornell University

— EAD. (1987) *Beloved*. New York, Penguin Books

— EAD. (1989) «Unspeakable Things Unspoken: The Afro-American Presence in American Literature». *Quarterly Review* 28: 1-34

— EAD. (1992) *Playing in the Dark: Whiteness and the Literary Imagination.* London, Picador

— EAD. (1993) *The Bluest Eye.* New York, Plume

— EAD. (2003) *Love.* London, Chattus and Windus

NEUMANN, E., (1981) (orig.1955) *The Great Mother,* London, Routledge

NEUSTADT, K., (1980) «The Visits of the Writers Toni Morrison and Eudora Welty», in *Conversations with Toni Morrison,* (eds.), Danielle Taylor- Guthrye, (1994) Mississippi, University Press of Mississippi: 84-92

NICHOLSON, C., (1992) *Knucklebones of Irony: Liz Lochhead,* in *Poem, Purpose and Place: Shaping Identity in Contemporary Scottish Verse,* Edinburgh, Polygon: 202-223

— ID. (2007) *Towards a Scottish Theatrocracy: Edwin Morgan and Liz Lochhead,* in Schoene, B. (eds.) *The Edinburgh Companion to Contemporary Scottish Literature,* Edinburgh, Edinburgh University Press: 159-166

NUSSBAUM, M., (1997) «Serpents in the Soul: A reading of Seneca's Medea», in *Medea: Essays on Medea in Myth, Literature and Art* (eds.) James Clauss and Sarah Iles Johnson, Princeton, N.J., Princeton University Press: 219-249

OSTRIKER, A.S., (1986) *Stealing the Language: The Emergence of Women's Poetry in America,* London, The Women's Press

OTTEN, T., (1991) *The Crime of Innocence in the Fiction of Toni Morrison,* Missouri, University of Missouri Press

PADUANO, G., (1968) *La formazione del mondo ideologico e poetico di Euripide. Al cesti, Medea,* Pisa, Nistri-Lischi, 1968

PARAT, H., (2003) *L'erotico materno: Psicoanalisi dell'allattamento,* Roma, Borla, (orig. 1999, *L'érotique maternelle: Psychanalyse de l'allaitement,* Paris, Dunod)

PEACH, L., (1995) *Toni Morrison,* London, McMillan

PENGLASE, C., (1994) *Greek Myths and Mesopotamia: Parallels and Influences in the Homeric Hymns and Hesiod.* New York, Routledge

PLASA, C., RING, B., (eds.), (1994) *The Discourse of Slavery,* London, Routledge

PLATO, (1984) *Dialogues* (transl. R. E. Allen) London, Yale University Press

— ID. *Republic,* G.R.F. Ferrari (eds.) (2000) Cambridge, Cambridge University Press

— ID. (2008) *Laws* (transl. R. Mayhew) Oxford, Clarendon University Press

POGGI, V.- ROSE, M. (eds.) (2000) *A Theatre that Matters: Twentieth-Century Scottish Drama and Theatre,* Milano, Unicopli

PORTELLI, A., (2004) *Canoni Americani,* Roma, Donzelli.

— ID. (1996) «Non era una Storia da Tralasciare», in Toni Morrison (1996), *Amatissima*, Milano, Frassinelli: 393-406

PUGLIESE, M., «Interview with Liz Lochhead» (unpublished, Edinburgh, 27 April 2009)

RAMAZZINI, B., *De Morbis Artificum Diatriba*, (Ultrajecti, 1703) 1982, Roma, Carocci

RANKE-GRAVES, R., (2011) *The Greek Myths*, London, Penguin (orig. 1955)

RANKINE, P., (2006) *Ulysses in Black. Ralph Ellison, Classicism and African American Literature*. Wisconsin, The University of Wisconsin Press

REINHOLD M., (1984) *Classica Americana: The Greek and Roman Heritage in the United States*. Detroit, Mich, Wayne State University Press

RICH, A., (1986) *Of Woman Born: Motherhood as Experience and Institution*, New York, Norton (orig. 1977)

RICOEUR, P., (1992) *Oneself as Another* (orig. 1990), Chicago, The University of Chicago Press

ROSE, M.- SONCINI, S., (2001) *Caledonia Dreaming. La Nuova Drammaturgia Scozzese*, Salerno, Oedipus

RONNICK, M.V., (eds.) (2005) The Autobiography of William Sanders Scarborough: *An American Journey from Slavery to Scholarship*. Detroit, Wayne State University Press

ROYNON, T., (2007a) «Toni Morrison and Classical Tradition». *Literature Compass*, 4/6: 1514-37

— EAD. (2007b) «A New »Romen» Empire: Toni Morrison's *Love* and the Classics». *Journal of American Studies*, 41/1: 31-47

RUAS, C., (1981) Toni Morrison, in *Conversations with Toni Morrison*, (eds.), Danielle Taylor- Guthrye, (1994) Mississippi, University Press of Mississippi: 93-118

SCARPA, G. (1994) «Toni Morrison: la Memoria, i Fantasmi e la Scrittura». Acoma: 68-77

SCULLION, A., *Self and the Nation: Issues of Identity in Modern Scottish Drama by Women*, New Theatre Quarterly: 68: 373-390

— EAD. (2002) *Contemporary Scottish Drama*, in Gifford, D. – Dunnigan, S. and MacGillivray, A. (eds.) *Scottish Literature*, Edinburgh, Edinburgh University Press: 794-833

SEGRE, C., (1985) *Tema / Motivo in Avviamento all'analisi del Testo letterario*, Torino, Einaudi: 331-359

SIMPSON J.A. and WEINER, E.S.C. (eds.) (1989) *OED, The Oxford English Dictionary*, (2nd edn, 20 vols), Oxford, Clarendon Press

SMITH, D.,(1998) *1950 to 1995*, in Findlay, B. (eds.) *A History of Scottish Theatre*, Edinburgh, Polygon: 253-308

SNOWDEN, F.M. Jr. (1970) *Blacks in Antiquity: Ethiopians in the Greco-Roman Experience*. Cambridge, Mass, Harvard University Press

— ID. (1983) *Before Color Prejudice: The Ancient View of Blacks.* Cambridge, Mass, Harvard University Press

SOLLORS, W., (1993), *The Return of Thematic Criticism*, London, Harard University Press

— ID. (1997) *Neither Black nor White yet Both: Thematic Exploration of Interracial Literature*, Oxford University Press

SOMERVILLE-ARJAT, G.- WILSON, R.E. (eds.) (1990) *Sleeping with Monsters. Conversations with Scottish and Irish Women Poets*, Edinburgh, Polygon

SPLENDORE, P., (2004) «Bad Daughters and Unmotherly Mothers. The New Family Plot in the Contemporary English Novel», in Adalgisa Giorgio (eds.) *Writing Mothers and Daughters. Renegotiating the Mother in Western European Narratives by Women*, New York, Berghahn Books: 185-214

STEVENSON, R.- WALLACE, K. (eds.) (1996) *Scottish Theatre since the Seventies*, Edinburgh, Edinburgh University Press

STOPPATO, A., (1887) *Infanticidio e procurato aborto. Studio di dottrina, legislazione e giurisprudenza penale*, Verona-Padova, 1887

TEDESCHI, C., (2010), *Commento alla Medea di Euripide*, Trieste: 8-35

TODD, E.B., *Liz Lochhead*, in *Verse*, 8.3 and 9.1 (Winter/Spring 1991), repbl. in Crawford, R. et al (eds.) *Talking Verse* (St. Andrews: Verse, 1995: 83-95)

TROUSSON, R., (1965) *Un Problèm de Literatur Compareè; les ètudes de thèmes: essai de mèthodologie*, Paris, Minard

VARTY, A., (1997) *The Mirror of the Vamp: Liz Lochhead*, in Gifford, D.- McMillan, D. (eds.) *A History of Scottish Women's Writing*, Edinburgh, Edinburgh University Press: 641-658

WALKER, T., (1983) *In Search of Our Mothers' Gardens*, Fort Washington, Harvest Books

WALTERS, T., (2007) *African American Literature and the Classicist Tradition. Black Women Writers from Wheately to Morrison.* New York, Palgrave

WEISEBURGER, S., (1998) *Modern Medea. A Family Story of Slavery and Child-murder from the Old South*, New York, Hill & Wang

WHEATLEY, P., (1773) *Poems on Various Subjects Religious and Moral*, London

— EAD. (1989) *The Poems of Phillis Wheatley*, (eds.), Julian D. Mason. Chapel Hill, The University of North Carolina Press

YOUNG, D., (1946) *«Plastic Scots» and the Scottish Literary Tradition*, Glasgow, McLellan

Web References

«Didaskalia, Ancient Theatre Today», «Panel Discussion on Complex Electra», Peterhouse College, Cambridge, 13-14 October 2001), 5.3, (Summer 2002), http://www.didaskalia.net/issues/vol5no3/trans 02.html last access 5th March 2013)

GRAZIANO, G., (magister Gratianus), *Decretum Gratiani (Concordantia discordantium canonum)*, in *Corpus Iuris Canonici* (eds. Ludwig Richter), Akademische Druk, Graz 1959, 2 voll. (vol. 1, coll. 1143 e 1162, http://geschichte.digitale-sammlungen.de/decretum-gratiani/online /angebot, last access 5th March, 2013)

HYSLOP, Fiona, MSP, Minister for Culture and External Affairs: *Response to the Literature Working Group report,* http://www.scotland.gov .uk/Resource/Doc/340871/0113157.pdf (last access 6th March, 2013)

IACONO, A., (2004) «Autonomia nella Relazione». *Polemos* (http:// www.polemos.it/paper/iacono2.doc last access 5th March, 2013)

LOCAL GOVERNMENT ACT (1988) (http://www.legislation.gov.uk /ukpga/1988/9/part/IV last access 6th march, 2013)

PARLIAMENT AND CONSTITUTION CENTRE, (2004) Devolution in Scotland, Standard Note House of Commons Library, (http://www.parliament.uk/documents/commons/lib/research/br iefings/snpc-03000.pdf, last access 5th March, 2013)

RONNICK, M.V., (1997) «After Bernal and Mary Lefkowitz: Research Opportunities in Classica Africana». *Negro History Bullettin 60*: 1-12; (http://department.monm.edu/Classics/cpl/PromotionalMaterials /Africana.htm, last access 5th March, 2013)

SCOTTISH ARTS COUNCIL, (2001) *Scottish National Theatre: Report of the Independent Working Group* (http://www.scottisharts.org.uk/1/ latestnews/1001911.aspx, last access 5th March, 2013)

— (Edinburgh, 24 July 2001) *A National Theatre for Scotland to be proud of* (http://www.sac.org.uk/1/latestnews/1001891.aspx, last access 6th March, 2013)

— (Edinburgh, September 2001) *Project and Lottery Grants* (http:// www.scottisharts.org.uk/resources/publications/past_awards/pdf/ AwardedGrantsSep01.pdf, last access 5thy March, 2013)

— *International Interest in Scottish translations* (Edinburgh, 28 March 2003) (http://www.scottisharts.org.uk/1/latestnews/1000724.aspx, last access 5th March, 2013)

SCOTTISH EXECUTIVE, (Edinburgh, 2000) *Creating Our Future, Minding Our Past: Scotland's National Cultural Strategy* (http://www.scot land.gov.uk/Resource/Doc/158792/0043111.pdf, last access 5th March, 2013)

Scottish Government, (2001) National Theatre of Scotland, (http://www.scotland.gov.uk/Publications/2003/11/18580/29640, last access 6th March, 2013)

(2003) Scotland's National Cultural Strategy Annual report, http://www.scotland.gov.uk/Publications/2003/11/18580/29640, last access 6th March, 2013)

van Binsbergen, D., (2004) Atena Nera? Prometeo: Rivista trimestrale di scienze e storia, 22. 85 (102-111); (http://www.shikanda.net/af rocentrism/prometeo.pdf, last access 5th March, 2013)

Lightning Source UK Ltd.
Milton Keynes UK
UKHW022322040521
383127UK00010B/2285